LEGAL RESPONSIBILITIES

of Nonprofit Boards

Second Edition

Bruce R. Hopkins, JD, LLM

BOARDSOURCE®

Building Effective Nonprofit Boards

Library of Congress Cataloging-in-Publication Data

Hopkins, Bruce R.

Legal responsibilities of nonprofit boards / Bruce R. Hopkins,
JD, LLM. -- 2nd ed.

    p. cm. -- (Governance series ; bk. 2)

ISBN 1-58686-107-7

1. Nonprofit organizations--Law and legislation--United States.
2. Charitable uses, trusts, and foundations--United States.
3. Boards of directors--Legal status, laws, etc.--United States.
4. Tort liability of charitable organizations--United States. I.
Title. II. Series.

      KF1388.7.H67 2008
      346.73'064--dc22   2008038861

© 2009 BoardSource.
First Printing, October 2008
ISBN 1-58686-107-7

Published by BoardSource
750 9th Street, NW, Suite 650
Washington, DC 20001

BOARDSOURCE®
Building Effective Nonprofit Boards

BoardSource was established in 1988 by the Association of Governing Boards of Universities and Colleges (AGB) and Independent Sector (IS). Prior to this, in the early 1980s, the two organizations had conducted a survey and found that although 30 percent of respondents believed they were doing a good job of board education and training, the rest of the respondents reported little, if any, activity in strengthening governance. As a result, AGB and IS proposed the creation of a new organization whose mission would be to increase the effectiveness of nonprofit boards.

With a lead grant from the Kellogg Foundation and funding from five other donors, BoardSource opened its doors in 1988 as the National Center for Nonprofit Boards with a staff of three and an operating budget of $385,000. On January 1, 2002, BoardSource took on its new name and identity. These changes were the culmination of an extensive process of understanding how we were perceived, what our audiences wanted, and how we could best meet the needs of nonprofit organizations.

Today BoardSource is the premier voice of nonprofit governance. Its highly acclaimed products, programs, and services mobilize boards so that organizations fulfill their missions, achieve their goals, increase their impact, and extend their influence. BoardSource is a 501(c)(3) organization.

BoardSource provides

- resources to nonprofit leaders through workshops, training, and an extensive Web site (www.boardsource.org)

- governance consultants who work directly with nonprofit leaders to design specialized solutions to meet an organization's needs

- the world's largest, most comprehensive selection of material on nonprofit governance, including a large selection of books and CD-ROMs

- an annual conference that brings together approximately 900 governance experts, board members, and chief executives and senior staff from around the world

For more information, please visit our Web site at www.boardsource.org, e-mail us at mail@boardsource.org, or call us at 800-883-6262.

Have You Used These BoardSource Resources?

THE GOVERNANCE SERIES

1. Ten Basic Responsibilities of Nonprofit Boards, Second Edition
2. Legal Responsibilities of Nonprofit Boards, Second Edition
3. Financial Responsibilities of Nonprofit Boards, Second Edition
4. Fundraising Responsibilities of Nonprofit Boards, Second Edition
5. The Nonprofit Board's Role in Mission, Planning, and Evaluation, Second Edition
6. Structures and Practices of Nonprofit Boards, Second Edition

BOOKS

The Nonprofit Legal Landscape

The Nonprofit Board's Guide to Bylaws

Managing Conflicts of Interest: A Primer for Nonprofit Boards, Second Edition

The Nonprofit Policy Sampler, Second Edition

Understanding Nonprofit Financial Statements, Third Edition

Chief Executive Transitions: How to Hire and Support a Nonprofit CEO

Chief Executive Succession Planning: The Board's Role in Securing Your Organization's Future

Assessment of the Chief Executive

The Board Chair Handbook, Second Edition

Getting the Best from Your Board: An Executive's Guide to a Successful Partnership

Moving Beyond Founder's Syndrome to Nonprofit Success

The Source: Twelve Principles of Governance That Power Exceptional Boards

Exceptional Board Practices: The Source in Action

Fearless Fundraising for Nonprofit Boards, Second Edition

Navigating the Organizational Lifecycle: A Capacity-Building Guide for Nonprofit Leaders

Driving Strategic Planning: A Nonprofit Executive's Guide

Taming the Troublesome Board Member

The Nonprofit Dashboard: A Tool for Tracking Progress

Meet Smarter: A Guide to Better Nonprofit Board Meetings

The Nonprofit Board Answer Book: A Practical Guide for Board Members and Chief Executives, Second Edition

Self-Assessment for Nonprofit Governing Boards

Transforming Board Structure: Strategies for Committees and Task Forces

The Board Building Cycle: Nine Steps to Finding, Recruiting, and Engaging Nonprofit Board Members, Second Edition

Culture of Inquiry: Healthy Debate in the Boardroom

DVDs

Meeting the Challenge: An Orientation to Nonprofit Board Service

Speaking of Money: A Guide to Fundraising for Nonprofit Board Members

For an up-to-date list of publications and information about current prices, membership, and other services, please call BoardSource at 800-883-6262 or visit our Web site at www.boardsource.org.

CONTENTS

ABOUT THE BOARDSOURCE GOVERNANCE SERIES

As BoardSource celebrated its 20th anniversary in 2008, we introduced updated editions of the books in the Governance Series, BoardSource's flagship series created to help nonprofit board members understand their primary roles and responsibilities. BoardSource believes that board members and chief executives who know and understand their mutual responsibilities are better equipped to advance their organizations' missions and, in turn, strengthen their communities.

WHY IS A STRONG BOARD IMPORTANT?

There's no denying that the 1.6 million nonprofit organizations in the United States play a vital role in society, from assisting victims of natural disasters to beautifying our neighborhoods, from educating our children to healing the sick. To ensure that their organizations have the resources, leadership, and oversight necessary to carry out these and other vital activities, nonprofit boards must understand and fulfill their governance responsibilities.

Although there have been headline-worthy scandals by a few nonprofits and their boards, the vast majority try hard every day to be worthy of the public's trust. Nevertheless, BoardSource frequently hears from nonprofit board members and chief executives who say that they are not always sure what the basic components of good governance are or how to educate every board member in them so they can serve their organizations and the public in the best possible manner. The revised Governance Series helps bridge this gap in knowledge.

Within the board's broad roles of setting the organization's direction, ensuring necessary resources, and providing oversight, board members wear many hats. They are guardians of the mission; they ensure compliance with legal and financial requirements; and they enforce ethical guidelines for their organization. They are policymakers, fundraisers, ambassadors, partners with the chief executive, and strategic thinkers. They monitor progress, evaluate the performance of the organization and the chief executive, and demonstrate integrity in everything they do on behalf of the organization. Because of their many roles, board members need more than enthusiasm for a cause, passion for a mission, or just "good intentions." They need to understand all of their stewardship responsibilities and perform all of their duties.

WHAT WILL BOARD MEMBERS FIND IN THE BOOKS?

The six books address all of the fundamental elements of service common to most boards, including board member responsibilities, how to structure the board in the most efficient manner, and how to accomplish governance work in the spirit of the mission of the organization.

1. *Ten Basic Responsibilities of Nonprofit Boards, Second Edition* (Book 1) by Richard T. Ingram describes the 10 core areas of board responsibility.

2. *Legal Responsibilities of Nonprofit Boards, Second Edition* (Book 2) by Bruce R. Hopkins, JD, LLM, elaborates on the board's legal responsibilities, liabilities, and the oversight it should provide to protect the organization.

3. *Financial Responsibilities of Nonprofit Boards, Second Edition* (Book 3) by Andrew S. Lang, CPA, explains board fiduciary responsibilities in the areas of financial oversight and risk management.

4. *Fundraising Responsibilities of Nonprofit Boards, Second Edition* (Book 4) by James M. Greenfield, ACFRE, FAHP, helps board members understand why they should be actively engaged in ensuring adequate resources for the organization — and how to get involved in fundraising.

5. *The Nonprofit Board's Role in Mission, Planning, and Evaluation, Second Edition* (Book 5) by Kay Sprinkel Grace, MA, Amy McClellan, MNO, and John A. Yankey, PhD, shows how to define and communicate the organization's mission and link strategic planning and evaluation to achieve organizational success.

6. *Structures and Practices of Nonprofit Boards, Second Edition* (Book 6) by Charles F. Dambach, MBA, Melissa Davis, and Robert L. Gale offers guidance on how to build and structure the board (size, committees, term limits) and enhance leadership roles and the partnership between the chair and the chief executive.

Each book focuses on one topic, breaking information into manageable amounts that are easy to digest. Readers will find real-world examples that provide insight from effective boards, statistics from BoardSource's *Nonprofit Governance Index 2007* survey of nonprofit organizations, tips and pitfalls, lists of the most important things to remember, end-of-chapter questions, glossaries, and resource lists for further reading. The authors of the books are subject matter experts with years of experience in the nonprofit sector.

WHO SHOULD READ THE BOOKS?

Board members and senior staff, especially chief executives, in nonprofits of all types and sizes will find the information contained in the Governance Series relevant. They can use it to set standards, to develop their own approaches to board work and interacting with board members, and to modify practices as the organization evolves.

There's something in the Governance Series for everyone associated with the board. A board chair, for example, might share Book 5 (*The Nonprofit Board's Role in Mission, Planning, and Evaluation*) with board members before starting a strategic planning process or give Book 4 (*Fundraising Responsibilities of Nonprofit Boards*) to the development committee. Chief executives will find it beneficial to give Book 3 (*Financial Responsibilities of Nonprofit Boards*) to the board treasurer and to review Book 1 (*Ten Basic Responsibilities of Nonprofit Boards*) and give it, along with Book 6 (*Structures and Practices of Nonprofit Boards*), to senior staff and the board chair to clarify board–chief executive roles and strengthen the partnership with the board. All board members will want to read Book 2 (*Legal Responsibilities of Nonprofit Boards*) so they understand how to protect themselves and the organization. The chair of the governance committee might give new board members all six books. This sharing helps ensure that everyone associated with the board is "on the same page" and has a common understanding of the board's responsibilities, expectations, and activities.

Board service entails serious obligations, to be sure, but it can also deliver immense satisfaction. A board that knows what is expected of it and performs at the highest level is a strategic resource for its organization and chief executive. And ultimately, this commitment by dedicated board members translates into mission impact in our communities.

The Governance Series was made possible in part through the support of MetLife Foundation.

INTRODUCTION

REASONABLENESS AND PRUDENCE

When joining the board of a nonprofit organization, you take on a set of responsibilities and duties defined by law. Along with attention to programs, finances, and fundraising, nonprofit board members should understand the regulatory environment in which their organizations operate. Fundamental legal principles and complex tax laws govern the work of nonprofit boards and board members.

Nonprofit organizations and their boards do not function in a vacuum. They are important players in the country's societal, economic, and legal framework and must adapt to — and sometimes act as the impetus for — environmental change. Other times, they may fulfill obligations and expectations common in the for-profit and government sectors.

For example, enactment of the Sarbanes-Oxley Act of 2002, passed by the U.S. Congress in the aftermath of various corporate and accounting firm scandals, raised the standards of scrutiny in the private sector for matters such as auditor independence, corporate responsibility, financial disclosure, and conflicts of interest. Aspects of this heightened concern for accountability have carried over into the nonprofit sector, more by practice than by legal requirements.

Thus, the board of a nonprofit organization is challenged with two seemingly contradictory mandates — advancing the good work of the organization and deciding the extent of its accountability to the public. This tension makes board service both difficult and rewarding.

FULFILLING FIDUCIARY RESPONSIBILITIES

Fundamental to the legal aspects of board membership is the concept of fiduciary responsibility. The control of a nonprofit organization is usually vested in its governing body, typically called the board of directors. The members of this board, charged with exercising responsibility over the organization and its resources, are considered fiduciaries. This concept of fiduciary responsibility extends to the accountability board members have assumed to both advance their organization's mission and oversee its assets.

Fiduciaries are held to a standard known as the test of reasonableness and prudence. This centuries-old test has its basis in English common law and the standards developed concerning governance of charitable trusts. In contemporary terms, this standard means that board members are expected to regard and treat the nonprofit organization's assets and other resources with the same care with which they would treat their own resources.

Because the board of directors is ultimately responsible for a nonprofit organization's activities, it often becomes the prime target when problems arise. The general argument often made against boards in these circumstances — and the one against which board members should defend themselves — is guilt by omission. This situation arises when board members have been passive or otherwise inactive in overseeing the activities of the nonprofit organization and, consequently, may have failed to adhere to the standards of fiduciary responsibility. To protect against these charges, board members must demonstrate that they appropriately discharged the requisite duties. Ignorance is not an acceptable excuse when a legal problem demands the board's attention.

GETTING SOUND ADVICE

Charged with oversight, board members inevitably struggle with the limitations created by their part-time (at best) involvement and their volunteer status. No board member can know everything. Boards must rely, to various extents, on independent professionals that the organization may retain.

Acknowledging that sound legal advice requires legal counsel, most organizations make considerable use of lawyers. An organization may have an ongoing relationship with one or more lawyers, who may be in private practice or employed by the organization. The lawyer may serve as a volunteer (perhaps as a board member) or be compensated (at full or reduced rates) for services rendered. In any case, board members should have access to the organization's lawyer, within reason; legal fees can mount if access to the lawyer is not monitored and limited.

Some organizations have their lawyer present at every meeting of the board or at least a portion of the meeting (sometimes with staff not present). Others have a lawyer available by telephone, should a question involving a legal matter arise. Some have their lawyer review drafts of board meeting minutes and/or annual information returns. A few organizations have a periodic legal audit.

The matter of lawyers on the board is tricky business. Like all of the other board members, the lawyers serve primarily as fiduciaries. Their role is not simply to provide free services for the board or the organization but to bring a new perspective and exercise vigilance. Although they will certainly speak up in the face of legal issues that come before the board, to the extent that those issues are within their range of expertise, board members with legal experience are not a substitute for the use of inside or outside legal counsel. Lawyers are sometimes asked to give opinions on the propriety of a board action, so having a lawyer on the board may put that lawyer in the awkward position of passing judgment on his or her own actions.

Also, most lawyers today specialize, so a lawyer on the board is not necessarily competent to advise an organization on nonprofit law. Finally, having a lawyer on the board — even one who specializes in nonprofit law — does not absolve the rest of the board members from being aware of their own responsibilities and duties under the law.

An understanding of the basic concepts and rules can go a long way toward helping a board member avoid personal liability. Simply put, board members need to ask

- What kind of oversight and policy judgments am I expected to provide and make?

- When and how can I be found personally liable?

- How can I avoid, or at least minimize, personal liability?

This book provides a starting point for answering these questions. While it offers a preliminary understanding of the legal landscape you must navigate as a member of a nonprofit board, this book does not and cannot substitute for the counsel of trained professionals.

Chapter 1 discusses the concept of fiduciary responsibility and the collective duties of care, loyalty, and obedience. Chapter 2 delves into the different forms that nonprofit organizations can take and describes how board members are elected. Chapter 3 summarizes the strategies for protecting board members from personal liability, while Chapter 4 outlines the policies and procedures that, increasingly, are becoming best practices within the nonprofit sector. The Conclusion offers some important things to remember when trying to minimize liability.

A list of discussion questions appears at the end of each chapter. These questions are designed to prompt board dialogue, either during a board retreat or at regular times set aside on the board meeting agenda. The Appendix presents several samples of recommended board policies, which may be adapted for use in any nonprofit. This book also offers a glossary of legal terms and concepts that apply to nonprofit organizations.

1

CHAPTER 1

LEGAL DUTIES OF THE BOARD AND BOARD MEMBERS

Hundreds of years ago, out of the common law of England, the concept evolved of legal entities being separate from individual human beings. This distinction, initially made to place income-producing assets in separate vehicles, gave rise to the legal fiction of discrete, recognized "persons." Later came the idea that legal liability could potentially be attached to these separate entities. Today, we know these entities as corporations, associations, partnerships, limited liability companies, estates, and the like.

In the beginning was the trust; next came charitable trusts. The contemporary law regarding the responsibilities of directors of nonprofit organizations is grounded in the common-law rules for administrators of charitable trusts. Directors today are fiduciaries of the organization's resources and guardians of its mission. In certain circumstances, responsibility traces back to the individual board member, who can be held liable for some actions undertaken in the organization's name and may have to pay penalties.

BOARD MEMBERS AS FIDUCIARIES

In charitable trusts, board members have the same obligation toward the trust's assets as they do toward their personal assets. Equally, all board members have the responsibility to act prudently in their handling of the nonprofit organization's resources. The trustees are fiduciaries; the law imposes on them standards of conduct and management that, together, constitute fiduciary responsibility.

Most state laws, by statute or court opinion, impose the standards of fiduciary responsibility on directors of nonprofit organizations, whether or not the organizations are trusts (and often whether or not they are charitable). Thus, personal liability can result when a board member, officer, or key employee of a nonprofit organization breaches the standards of fiduciary responsibility.

A chief responsibility of board members is to maintain financial accountability and effective oversight of the organization they serve. As trustees of the organization's assets, board members must exercise due diligence to see that the organization is well managed and that its financial situation remains sound. Fiduciary duty requires board members to be objective, unselfish, responsible, honest, trustworthy, and efficient.

Board members, as stewards of the organization's resources, should always act for the good of the organization, rather than for their personal benefit. They need to exercise reasonable care in all decision making, without placing the organization under unnecessary risk.

COLLECTIVE AND SHARED RESPONSIBILITIES

The distinction of legal liability between the board and an individual board member relates to the responsibility of *the board* for the organization and responsibility of *individual board members* for their actions. The board as a collective entity is responsible and liable for what happens in and to the organization. As the ultimate authority, it must ensure that the organization operates in compliance with the law and its own policies.

Boards make decisions in a legally structured meeting. One critical element of a legal meeting is the presence of a quorum — the minimum number of voting members who need to be present before the meeting can take place. The quorum should be defined as the reasonable number of board members who can attend a meeting at any given time. If the quorum is defined with less demanding parameters and a majority vote of those present is required, it is possible that a few board members will end up making major decisions for the organization.

If legal action ensues, it can often be traced to an inattentive, passive, or captive board. For example, an attorney general may proceed against a public charity for payment of excessive compensation to an executive, even when the board was entirely unaware of the compensation arrangement. Or the organization may be involved in employment discrimination or the making of defamatory statements, with the board wholly in the dark as to the practices.

To avoid legal action, board members should attend meetings regularly; make independent and justified decisions, rather than simply voting with the majority; and, before approving any meeting minutes, review the document carefully to ensure it truly reflects what happened in the meeting. As government regulators grow more aggressive in demanding accountability, boards must become correspondingly more vigilant and active in establishing and implementing sound policies.

PITFALL

When board members have difficulties attending meetings, it is tempting to lower the quorum requirements to be able to conduct meetings regularly. By accommodating the missing participants, however, not only does the board send the wrong message, fewer board members end up making important decisions. A better solution is to allow directors who cannot attend in person to join the meeting by telephone, which is allowed in every state (usually when authorized in the bylaws) and counts the same as presence in person.

In turn, the board's shared legal responsibilities depend on the actions of its individual members. All board members are liable for their own acts and deeds — particularly if those actions are alleged to be civil or even criminal offenses. In practice, this requires board members to hold each other accountable.

Board members do not, individually, have unilateral authority to make decisions about the organization's governance. Rather, the board has collective responsibilities, as emphasized by the U.S. Congress in 2007 when it passed legislation that amended the congressional charter of the American Red Cross. Aimed at modernizing the organization's structure and strengthening its governance, the legislation called for the American Red Cross to substantially reduce the size of its board, delegate day-to-day operations to management, eliminate distinctions regarding the election of board members, and form an advisory council.

Because the American Red Cross is a federally chartered organization, Congress was given the opportunity to enumerate the responsibilities listed below. These responsibilities are good reminders for nonprofit boards in general.

- Review and approve the organization's mission statement.

- Approve and oversee the organization's strategic plan and maintain strategic oversight of operational matters.

- Select, evaluate, and determine the level of compensation of the organization's chief executive officer.

- Evaluate the performance and establish the compensation of the senior leadership team and provide for management succession.

- Oversee the financial reporting and audit process, internal controls, and legal compliance.

- Ensure that the chapters of the organization (if any) are geographically and regionally diverse.

- Hold management accountable for performance.

- Provide oversight of the organization's financial stability.

- Ensure the inclusiveness and diversity of the organization.

- Provide oversight of the protection of the organization's brand. (This is a responsibility rarely found in a list of this nature.)

- Assist with fundraising on behalf of the organization.

As for determining compensation, board practices differ. Some boards are involved in setting the compensation only of the chief executive; others at least approve the compensation of the senior staff. At a minimum, however, boards should approve the items of compensation that appear on the organization's annual information return (Form 990).

THE THREE Ds

The duties of the board of directors of a nonprofit organization can be encapsulated in the three Ds: duty of care, duty of loyalty, and duty of obedience.

Defined by case law, these are the legal standards by which all actions taken by directors are judged. The entire board and individual board members must adhere to these collective duties. Boards demonstrate accountability by showing they have effectively discharged these three duties.

DUTY OF CARE

The duty of care requires that directors of a nonprofit organization be reasonably informed about the organization's activities, participate in decisions, and do so in good faith and with the care of an ordinarily prudent person in similar circumstances. In short, the duty of care requires the board — and individual board members — to pay attention to the organization's activities and operations.

The duty of care is carried out by

- attending board meetings and meetings of appropriate committees
- preparing in advance for board meetings, such as reviewing reports and the agenda before arriving at the meeting
- obtaining information, before voting, to make sound decisions
- exercising independent judgment
- periodically examining the credentials and performance of those who serve the organization
- frequently reviewing the organization's finances and financial policies

- ensuring compliance with state and federal filing requirements, particularly annual information returns

DUTY OF LOYALTY

The duty of loyalty requires board members to exercise their power in the interest of the organization and not in their own interest or the interest of another entity, particularly one with which they have a formal relationship. When acting on behalf of the organization, board members must put the interests of the organization before their personal and professional interests.

In practice, the duty of loyalty is carried out by

- adhering to the organization's conflict-of-interest policy

- disclosing any conflicts of interest

- avoiding the use of corporate opportunities for personal gain or benefit

- maintaining the confidentiality of information about the organization

Conflicts of interest are not inherently illegal — in fact, they are quite common because board members are often affiliated with many different entities in their communities. What's important is how the board handles them. Conflict-of-interest policies can help protect the organization and board members by establishing a process for disclosure and voting when board members may potentially derive personal or professional benefit from the organization's activities.

TIP

It is not always possible to list all the potential conflicts on a disclosure form. Many conflicts of interest are tied to a specific transaction or a decision that could not be anticipated. Each situation should be evaluated on the basis of its facts and circumstances.

A conflict of interest may occur, for example, when a lawyer serving as a director also provides legal services to the organization. The same may be the case with an accountant, fundraising consultant, or insurance provider. Conflicts can also arise where the organization procures goods or services from a company owned by a board member or a board member's family.

Even lawful conflicts may draw the criticism of regulators, community watchdogs, and the media. An organization that exhibits too much of this type of behavior may negatively affect the perceptions of prospective donors and otherwise erode its credibility within the community.

WHEN INTERESTS COLLIDE

A conflict of interest exists when a person with a significant relationship with the organization also derives benefit (or is in a position to derive benefit) from the organization's activities. A conflict of interest is not, in itself, illegal — it is normal and happens constantly. The important issue is how the board deals with it.

A conflict typically arises when an organization needs to purchase a good or a service and a board member, or a company owned by a board member, is a provider of that good or service. In one case, for example, a public charity needed the services of an architect; one of the principals in the architectural firm it hired was the son of the charity's board chair. The firm was amply competent to provide the necessary services, but the arrangement gave rise to a major problem of "appearance." A board of directors in this position must decide whether to live with the conflict (and likely endure criticism) or select another provider solely to avoid the problem.

Adopting a conflict-of-interest policy is not required as a matter of law. In fact, this type of policy is only legally required in the case of exempt hospitals, but the IRS is advocating this policy requirement as a condition of tax-exempt status for public charities. Consequently, a nonprofit organization — particularly a charitable one — should seriously consider instituting a conflict-of-interest policy. A sample conflict-of-interest policy recommended by the IRS can be found at the back of the instructions to IRS Form 1023, or on the Web at www.irs.gov/pub/irs-pdf/i1023.pdf. The Appendix of this book contains another example.

Illustrations of situations that might present a real, potential, or perceived conflict of interest within a nonprofit organization include

1. A popular middle school is considering expansion to serve grades K-12. Board members whose children would otherwise move on to another high school vote for the expansion even though the financial analysis does not support the decision.

2. Physicians serving on a hospital board also compete with each other for outpatient services.

3. A close personal friend of the organization's chief executive is being recruited as a board member.

4. A representative of a recipient of funds makes funding choices as a member of the board.

5. A museum trustee — as a private collector — attends an auction of rare objects that would also be ideal additions to the museum collection.

6. The chief executive serves on the board of a similar organization.

7. A board member serving on two boards is asked by both to solicit grants from the same foundation.

8. A board member who is a senior executive in a publicly traded company also serves on the nonprofit's investment committee. He highly recommends that the organization invest in his company.

9. After a board decides to compensate its members, the members themselves determine the amount that is appropriate (without independent advice).

10. A board member rents an office space to the organization at an advantageous price. During the following year, the full board approves major renovation to the premises.

11. A choreographer serving on a board of a dance company regularly has his work highlighted in the annual program; the artistic director orders a special work from the choreographer to celebrate the dance company's anniversary.

12. The organization grants annual volunteer awards. A board member recommends his daughter — a well-respected and active member of the community — as a recipient.

DUTY OF OBEDIENCE

The duty of obedience requires that directors of a nonprofit organization comply with applicable federal, state, and local laws, adhere to the organization's bylaws, and remain the guardians of the mission.

The duty of obedience is carried out by

- ensuring compliance with all regulatory and reporting requirements, such as filing the annual information return (usually, IRS Form 990) and paying employment taxes

- examining all documents that govern the organization and its operation, such as the bylaws

- making decisions that fall within the scope of the organization's mission and governing documents

Generally, directors who carry out their duties faithfully and in adherence to the three Ds will not be found personally liable. Unfortunately, however, there cannot be any guarantees. Remember: Individual responsibility and the responsibility of the board, as a whole, overlap. The demarcation can often be indistinct and, in legal action under certain circumstances, an individual board member may end up paying the penalties or being hit with other sanctions.

Say, for example, an organization fails to pay employment taxes (or taxes that should have been withheld). The organization's board members (or at least the officers responsible for employment and financial matters) are likely to be expected to personally make the appropriate payment to the IRS. As another example, board members who are directly involved in employment discrimination may be personally liable for damages.

QUESTIONS THE BOARD SHOULD ASK

1. Do we regularly have a quorum at board meetings?

2. If the bylaws have a policy about missing meetings (such as termination of the member's involvement), do we uniformly follow the policy?

3. Do all board members regularly receive and read information in advance of board meetings?

4. Do we refer to our mission statement as a guide when making decisions?

5. Do individual board members periodically review and sign our board's conflict-of-interest policy?

6. Who in our organization is responsible for keeping the legal documents?

7. Can we easily access legal documents if we need them?

CHAPTER 2

LEGAL CONTEXTS

Within the nonprofit sector, operating budgets range from next to nothing to billions of dollars. Organizational support may come from fees for service, contributions, grants, contracts, and even businesses that may or may not be related to the organization's mission. Some organizations have large professional staffs; others operate almost entirely with volunteers. Some attract the involvement of the community power structure; others take a strictly grassroots approach.

Regardless of its size and shape, a nonprofit must have a board of directors (sometimes known as a board of trustees). The board may be elected by the organization's membership, appointed by public authorities or other institutions, or self-perpetuating (meaning the board appoints member replacements). Some boards are large, numbering more than 50 or even 100 members. Others are small, with only one to three board members as allowed by the state's law.

Despite these differences, all boards of incorporated nonprofits must operate within the laws of the state in which the organization is incorporated (and in any other states where it "does business"). Boards are also accountable for the organization's legal and ethical conduct and, increasingly, donors — as well as the general public — demand that boards serve as responsible stewards of organizational resources.

Board business is serious business. Board members need to understand the way the law recognizes their authority levels and overall expectations vis-à-vis the organization.

PITFALL

Failing to clarify the expectations for all board members is like building a board without an action plan: You may have an impressive-looking board that seems to get along well but ends up accomplishing little.

TAX EXEMPTION

Nonprofit, often used as a layperson's term, has a legal meaning that reflects the organization's commitment to mission over profit and how any profits are used. It is perfectly acceptable for nonprofits to generate revenue in excess of expenses or strive for a sizable reserve fund to cover future expenses or plan for expansion. All revenue, however, must be used for the good of the organization. None of the revenue can benefit an individual or that person's affiliations — beyond payment of reasonable compensation for services.

As defined by Section 501(c) of the Internal Revenue Code, tax-exempt organizations generally do not have to pay federal income tax. Section 501(c) has many subcategories. The largest group is 501(c)(3)s, which are designated as charities and generally must benefit the public good. Because of this public service purpose (which often lightens a government's burden), contributions to these public charities are tax deductible to donors.

Private foundations provide funding to public charities, which in turn provide direct services to the community. Private foundations are often closely aligned with an individual, family, or corporation. They face greater tax and reporting burdens, including a requirement to annually pay out an amount equal to 5 percent of the amount of their net investment assets.

For most 501(c)(3) charitable organizations, the goal is to be recognized as a public charity rather than a private foundation — even if both can receive tax-deductible donations. Public charities administer their own programs rather than support other organizations and they can also engage in lobbying activities, whereas private foundations are more constrained in their attempts to influence legislation. (Both categories of charitable organizations are essentially prohibited from participating in political campaign activity.) On the other hand, public charities often must meet a test of public support to demonstrate a broad funding base, rather than depend on only one or a few sources.

Social welfare and public advocacy groups are often classified as 501(c)(4) organizations. Established to influence public policy, they, too, are generally exempt from paying income taxes. Because social welfare and public advocacy organizations participate in influencing government policy, their supporters cannot claim tax deductions for contributions.

Trade associations and professional societies are often classified as 501(c)(6) organizations. Established to promote the interests of particular professions or lines of business or trade, they generally do not pay taxes; contributions to them, however, are not tax deductible because they serve the interests of their members and not the public.

ORGANIZATIONAL FORM

A nonprofit organization is, usually by state law, a separate legal entity. This fundamental fact dictates that the entity have a form. Nonprofit organizations usually are corporations, unincorporated associations, or trusts.

CORPORATION

In the case of a corporation, liability is generally confined to the organization itself and does not normally extend to those who manage it (staff and board members). For this reason alone, most nonprofit organizations probably should be incorporated.

Incorporation has another advantage. The state incorporation law may provide answers to many of the questions — about board size, meeting requirements, and dissolution — that inevitably arise when forming and operating a nonprofit organization. The comfort factor also accounts for the prevalence of nonprofit corporations. Most people, from the IRS to private foundations, are familiar with corporations, which makes it easier for the organization to function in the business world.

Generally, the advantages of incorporation far outweigh the disadvantages. The most significant disadvantage stems from the fact that incorporation entails an affirmative act of the state government and carries certain restrictions. In exchange for providing a charter to the entity through its grant of corporate status, for instance, the state usually expects certain forms of compliance by the organization. This compliance may entail adherence to rules of operation, an initial filing fee, annual reports, and annual fees. These costs are frequently nominal; reporting requirements usually are not extensive.

Articles of incorporation clarify the main features of the organization: its purpose, mission, structure of authority, names of incorporators, registered agent, initial board members, and applicable federal tax law requirements. Bylaws articulate the corporate authority structure in more detail and outline the fundamental governance processes. They establish the rules that help provide legal protection to the board members.

Organizations may adopt operational policies and procedures in a separate formal document. These rules may be more freely amended than articles or bylaws. They should not, however, be inconsistent with the articles or bylaws but complement and add to them.

UNINCORPORATED ASSOCIATION

On the surface, a nonprofit corporation and a nonprofit unincorporated organization look alike. For example, a membership association has the same characteristics, whether or not it is incorporated. An unincorporated association, however, does not offer the shield against individual liability provided by the corporate form. It is not bound by state corporation laws.

Generally, an unincorporated association does not have to register with and annually report to a state (other than for fundraising purposes). This freedom from reporting constitutes one of its principal advantages vis-à-vis the corporation. Although the corporate form offers far more advantages, incorporating the organization may not be necessary when its mission and scope do not require a structure of complicated finances or serious liability protection. It may function instead as an informal group of volunteers. For instance, many hobby groups, garden societies, and other affinity groups may be good candidates for the unincorporated association status: They desire some collective guidelines for the members but do not need the strict rules of state laws.

An unincorporated association is formed by the adoption of a constitution. The contents of a constitution and articles of incorporation are much the same; the contents of bylaws of an unincorporated association are usually the same as those of a nonprofit corporation.

TRUST

A nonprofit organization may be formed as a trust. Some private foundations, for example, are trusts. (Those created by a will are known as testamentary trusts.) This is rarely an appropriate form for a nonprofit organization other than a philanthropic entity. The trustees of a trust do *not* have the protection against personal liability afforded by the corporate form.

Most state laws concerning trusts are written for the regulation of charitable trusts. These rules are rarely as flexible as desired by contemporary nonprofit organizations, and they frequently impose fiduciary standards that are more stringent than those for nonprofit corporations. On the other hand, the trust form may be used to protect the founder's privacy because a trust can be created without filing with the state. Thus, with the trust form, the identity of the governing board, and perhaps the amount of assets and funding, may be shielded from public view; this aspect of the law varies from state to state. Also, with the trust form, it is considerably more difficult for the board of trustees to change the purposes of the organization, thereby providing greater protection for the founder's donative intent. In some instances, the reporting obligations imposed on a trust are much less stringent than those imposed on corporations.

A nonprofit corporation taking the form of a trust requires the execution of a trust agreement or a declaration of trust. It is unusual — although certainly permissible — for the trustee(s) of a trust to adopt a set of bylaws.

BOARD MEMBERS

According to the law in most states, a nonprofit corporation must have at least three directors (or trustees). A few states require only one director. Although one size certainly does not fit all, it generally makes sense for the board to have between five and 20 members. According to BoardSource's *Governance Index 2007*, the average number of members on a board is 16. Having more members allows the board to have a concentration of talents and different perspectives, yet too many members can complicate board dynamics and reduce the opportunities for board members to interact with one another and the group in a meaningful manner.

Few nonprofit organizations have just one manager; in tax language, directors, officers, and key employees are *organization managers*. For purposes of this book, the emphasis is on the legal roles and responsibilities of directors, commonly referred to as the board. *Directors* generally oversee administration of the organization. The word *generally* is used because day-to-day management is supposed to be the province of employees. The directors are the policymakers of the organization; they develop plans for the organization and oversee its affairs.

The board may delegate the everyday management to the chief executive who, in turn and as the finances allow, may hire additional staff to help with the operations and administration. Depending on the organizational chart, various titles indicate the specific duties of employees regarding operations.

The board of directors may also delegate certain governance duties to officers, usually board members with additional leadership capacities. State laws generally define the overall officer duties. Officers may include a board chair or president, vice-chair or vice-president, secretary, treasurer, and chief executive. (For more information on officers, see *Structures and Practices of Nonprofit Boards*, Book 6 in the BoardSource Governance Series.)

In reality, it is difficult to precisely demarcate where the board's authority ends and the authority of the officers begins. The authority of directors and officers in relation to the authority of employees is equally hard to separate. All too frequently, authority is resolved on an occasion-by-occasion basis. To prevent contentious issues of territory, the board and chief executive should attempt to clarify boundaries through policies and procedures.

HOW BOARD MEMBERS ARE ELECTED

Rarely will a nonprofit organization have owners, although a few states permit stock-based nonprofit corporations. Control of a nonprofit organization, however, is another matter. A membership may control a nonprofit organization without owning it; more frequently, the board of directors controls a nonprofit organization, even one that has a membership. So, who serves on the board and how they become a primary part of the organization matter.

Board members may be elected by a general membership, elected by the existing board, appointed by a public official, or selected by virtue of their position. Boards may use some or all of these processes in defining their composition.

If the nonprofit organization has bona fide members, they will likely elect some or all of the members of the governing board. Election may be by mail ballot, online, or at an annual meeting. This election process is often used in trade associations, professional societies, and fraternal organizations. In the absence of a membership (or if the membership has no vote on the matter), the governing board may be self-perpetuating. That means the initial board appoints its successors, and the process continues as new members are added.

Particularly when an organization receives government funding or is closely affiliated with a parent organization, the outside or controlling authority may have the right to nominate one or more board members. This enables the outside authority to exert some influence and added oversight over how the organization functions and allocates its funds. These nominated board members are expected to fulfill the same basic responsibilities as the rest of the board, with the possible exception of government officials who may not be able to participate in fundraising.

TIP

However board members are elected — by current members of the board, members of the organization, or outside authorities — it is crucial to keep the governance committee involved in defining the board's needs and candidates' qualifications. The objective is always to build the most competent and committed board possible.

Self-perpetuating boards and membership-elected boards may have one or more ex officio positions. Ex officio simply means "by virtue of office or position." This term does not determine whether the person is a voting member of the board; the bylaws should clarify voting rights. Some boards specify ex officio positions for the chief executive, one or more past presidents, or people who hold positions in a separate but related organization (such as a supporting foundation or a parent organization). In some organizations, a public official is automatically an ex officio board member.

A board of directors of a nonprofit organization usually acts by means of in-person meetings at which a quorum must be present. Where state law allows, the members of the board can act at a meeting held via a conference call, providing that all participants can hear each other, or by unanimous written consent. There is almost no law concerning online meetings of the board (as opposed to online voting by an organization's members). Applicable state law must be checked; certainly, e-mail discussions are not likely to be regarded under state laws as formal meetings.

These alternative procedures must also be authorized in the bylaws. Unless there is a specific authorization in the law, directors of a nonprofit organization may not vote by proxy, mail ballot, or telephone calls (other than a conference call).

OTHER BOARD STRUCTURES

The board creates committees to accomplish the work that needs to get done between board meetings. An organization's bylaws should specify permanent standing committees, provide for the possibility of creating other committees or task forces, and describe how committee members are appointed. Non–board members may serve on committees, and they do so without the threat of personal liability that may accrue to directors.

According to BoardSource's *Nonprofit Governance Index 2007,* the most common committees defined in an organization's bylaws are executive, finance, governance, development, and audit, with the rest convened at the recommendation of the full board. Board committees often debate and present options to the full board for action, but some committees (most commonly, development committees) act more independently by organizing special events and facilitating other fundraising efforts.

A board may create an advisory council — a group that does not substitute for the board of directors but provides specialized expertise with respect to the organization's programs. Such councils might, for example, provide independent program evaluation, expand outreach efforts, or gather feedback from the community. This approach allows the governing board to carry out its fiduciary responsibilities and tap into greater community resources. Also, an advisory council can allow the board to surround itself with prominent names in the field or benefit from those who possess specialized expertise.

TIP

Consider having your board members fill out and sign personal commitment forms, thus encouraging them to individualize their participation. Board members tend to be more engaged when they have had a say in their own activities rather than having them dictated by someone else.

Because members of advisory councils lack voting rights, their number is governed only by what is practical. Unlike governing board members, advisory group members have no legal or formal responsibilities. Corporate law does not give them a specific status: They have no vested right to serve, no immunity from removal, and no right to renewal or appointment.

To avoid misleading implications that the advisory council has the power to make policy, limit its actions to

- making recommendations
- providing background for board decisions
- furnishing pros and cons for issues
- listing questions that are appropriate for the situation
- carrying out specific tasks

Reports issued by the advisory council should reflect any minority opinions. The board does not have to follow the advisory council's advice, but it should recognize the council's input out of respect and consideration to its members.

 ## QUESTIONS THE BOARD SHOULD ASK

1. Do we have a copy of our state laws, and are we operating in concordance with all the statutes?

2. When did we last review our bylaws? Are there any provisions we should add or delete?

3. Have we clearly defined the voting rights of any ex officio members of the board?

4. Do our bylaws clarify the election process for new board members and officers?

5. Do we have job descriptions for our committees that also define the limits of their authority?

CHAPTER 3
MANAGING LEGAL LIABILITY

Liability is closely tied to accountability. The issues most likely to arouse concern pertain to general ethical behavior, transparency (how the organization shares information), and money-related issues — ensuring that spending is aligned with donor intent, monitoring executive compensation, and expending money efficiently without waste.

Today, the concept of fiduciary responsibility is such that directors of nonprofit organizations can be found personally liable for a violation of that responsibility. When an individual is personally sued because of something done — or not done — in the name of a nonprofit organization, the potential liability is called personal liability.

A key step in liability protection is to know where the danger lies. The most common reasons why nonprofits get sued are

- employment claims (hiring, firing, contracts, benefits)
- contract claims (length of agreement, termination, work specification, payment terms)
- discrimination claims (employment, volunteers, programs)
- torts/negligence (injuries, theft)
- release of records (availability of corporate records)
- defamation

For the most part, the defendants in lawsuits involving nonprofit organizations are the organizations themselves. Seldom will the charges include other parties, such as individuals. These allegations can happen, however, and when they do, directors, officers, and key employees — perhaps even those acting as volunteers — can be dragged into the fray.

In most cases, the conduct of employees (when they are serving as employees of the organization) is considered conduct by the organization itself. If an employee's action (or lack of it) is outside the scope of employment, however, the individual can be held personally liable. If the board has not carried out its oversight duties adequately, it may be implicated in a lawsuit due to negligence of its duty of care (see Chapter 1).

PITFALL

Asking questions about board business via e-mail can bring quick responses but also easily evolve into evidence used to attack someone or charge him with an offense — especially if the messages are carelessly worded. Just remember: Lawyers think of e-mail as "exhibit mail."

To be legitimately named as a defendant, a person must have some involvement in the particular facts that go beyond the usual role of a board member. For example, a board member may be substantively involved in causing an employee to be fired and thus personally named in a lawsuit asserting employment discrimination. Or, if a board member made specific statements in the context of a contract negotiation, that person can end up as a defendant in a breach-of-contract lawsuit. And, anyone making a defamatory statement in the capacity of a board member, along with the organization, may be sued for damages.

TIP

Develop a policy requiring the organization's lawyer (particularly outside counsel) to report to one or more board members if staff does not properly handle or resolve a legal matter.

FUNDAMENTAL PROTECTIVE STRATEGIES

The key to protection is proactive positive action. In other words, being a good board member — attending to substantive and procedural issues with the conscientiousness and attentiveness that likely drew each person to board membership in the first place — represents a giant step toward insulation from potential problems. Even with the best of intentions, however, the risk of personal liability for board members of nonprofit organizations cannot be eliminated. Still, it can be minimized.

In a litigious society, anybody can sue anybody; even frivolous cases cost money. The organization can undertake some fundamental protective strategies, and board members can implement an action program to help ward off or, if necessary, defend against personal liability.

Proactive Governance. The protective impact offered by the latest technology and carefully crafted insurance policies wanes if those in the boardroom lack a fundamental understanding of their responsibilities, respect of ethical guidelines, civil code of conduct, and general communication savvy.

First, a board must recognize the fundamental duties and responsibilities inherent in volunteer board service. Next, it must develop a basic understanding of the legal framework that surrounds the organization and its structure. Finally, all board members must show good intentions by being accountable for their own actions.

TIP

Use consent agendas to allow the board more time to deliberate on difficult issues. If time is not of the essence with a specific issue, it is wiser to table the discussion and make a more educated decision during the next board meeting after more research has been conducted. Airing all sides of an issue carefully is one way to protect board members later on.

Good intentions coupled with ignorance rarely serve as a solid support if board members must defend their actions — or lack of action — in court. To provide a strong base of security against lawsuits, boards should draft policies, ensure those policies are followed, refrain from delegating fiduciary duties, and rely on expert advice when a particular acumen is missing in the boardroom.

Incorporation. The main benefit of incorporation is the limited liability protection that it provides for the organization's managers and board members. The corporation assumes its debt and obligations. (See Chapter 2 for more information about nonprofit corporations.) Also, because a corporation normally exists in perpetuity and its status is not altered by changes of personnel, incorporation brings a stability that is a key element in risk management.

Indemnification. Indemnification means that one party promises to protect another party from losses resulting from risks while carrying out specified duties. State laws usually allow nonprofits to indemnify their board members or some of their actions.

Generally, board members are indemnified — usually as spelled out in the bylaws — by the organization against judgments (and legal fees) incurred when they are acting in the service of the organization. For example, a director may have signed a contract on behalf of the organization (acting in good faith) and subsequently become embroiled in a breach-of-contract lawsuit. Under certain circumstances, the nonprofit may indemnify the board member only for court costs and not for the judgment. Of course, indemnification cannot cover criminal acts and certain willful acts that violate civil law.

Providing indemnification must be a business decision for the nonprofit. Taking into account the potentially enormous sums that the organization might have to pay out, without additional insurance protection, the organizational assets may quickly disappear after one particularly consuming legal case. Simply put, indemnification is as good as the organization's capacity to pay. It is possible, however, to purchase insurance to cover indemnification obligations.

Immunity. Immunity is available when the law provides that a class of individuals, under certain circumstances, is not liable for a particular act or set of acts or for failure to undertake a particular act or set of acts.

The Volunteer Protection Act of 1997 was created to "provide certain protections to volunteers, nonprofit organizations, and governmental entities in lawsuits based on the activities of volunteers." While this legislation provides basic protection for the discharge of certain activities, it should not be construed as offering comprehensive umbrella coverage. It is also important to note that the Volunteer Protection Act does not protect the organization itself, which still may be held liable for the acts of its volunteers. Neither does it protect a volunteer from being named as a defendant in a lawsuit.

The act covers volunteers if they were acting within the framework of their duties, were properly licensed or certified, and met the minimum standards of conduct. They are not covered if they operated any motor vehicles, committed an act of violence, were convicted of sexual harassment, or acted under the influence of drugs or alcohol.

Several states have enacted immunity laws for officers and directors of nonprofit organizations, protecting them in case of assorted civil law violations, particularly where these individuals are functioning as volunteers. In one instance, a member of a nonprofit swim club slipped on a watery surface and was injured; an immunity law shielded the board members from personal liability.

PITFALL

The practice of providing even modest compensation to nonprofit board members may void their immunity from personal liability.

Insurance. Insurance coverage transfers the risk of liability to an independent third party — an insurance company. General liability policies cover negligent acts that result in property, personal, or bodily injury. The latter would include, for example, a slip-and-fall accident on a wet floor at a nonprofit organization's offices. Errors and Omissions policies cover harm resulting from executive decision making, such as actions taken in good faith by an officer or director on behalf of the organization (for example, purchasing an item or making an investment decision). Bonding protects an organization from wrongful financial actions, such as the treasurer absconding with the organization's funds (or other forms of embezzlement).

Employment-related suits are the most common suits with which nonprofits must deal. One major benefit of Directors' and Officers' (D&O) insurance is coverage for liabilities from employment practices, such as allegations of intentional acts. Typically, a D&O policy is a must for a nonprofit board. It reimburses the organization for any indemnification expenses it may have suffered and provides direct payments to those insured when the organization is not reimbursing them.

Rather than purchasing a standard D&O policy, evaluate the unique circumstances of the organization and carefully study its particular needs for protection. Questions to ask about D&O policies include

- Who is covered? (Are all board members, other volunteers, and key staff covered?)

- Who is excluded? (Will compensation of board members exclude them?)

- What is excluded? (Often the exclusion paragraphs are the largest of the policy.)

- How is loss defined? (For instance, if the office is destroyed, are loss of usage and rental fees considered losses?)

- Are lawyers' fees, all types of penalties, and punitive damages included?

- Are defense costs reimbursed or paid as incurred?

- Are past acts covered, or will former board members be excluded?

Other types of policies typically purchased by nonprofit organizations include conference or convention cancellation insurance, vehicle insurance, and individual "super" policies for board members. Certain risks, however — such as criminal law liability — cannot be shifted via insurance. The insurance contract will likely exclude from coverage certain forms of civil law liability, such as libel and slander, intended employee discrimination, and antitrust matters because these generally relate to intentional acts. Even where adequate coverage is available, insurance today can be costly; premiums can easily total thousands of dollars annually, even with a sizable deductible.

QUESTIONS THE BOARD SHOULD ASK

1. Does our board periodically (at least every two to three years) review its insurance coverage to make sure it remains adequate and up-to-date?

2. Has the board ensured that the personnel policies include all the necessary clauses to help protect us from the most common legal actions?

3. Do we have an insurance policy that covers any indemnification costs if we ever had to indemnify a board member?

4. Does our D&O insurance cover defense costs as incurred or not until the proceedings are over?

CHAPTER 4
GOVERNANCE POLICIES AND ISSUES

Governance issues dominate the nonprofit law scene, as illustrated by two important developments in recent years. First, the Panel on the Nonprofit Sector in 2007 promulgated a set of principles of nonprofit governance. And, in 2008, the IRS introduced a redesigned Form 990, the annual information return filed by most tax-exempt organizations.

The objective of these guidelines and recommendations is to introduce good, ethical practices so that government doesn't have to step in and regulate all organizations in the same fashion, without regard to the enormous diversity within the nonprofit sector. These guidelines encourage individual boards to draft policies and practices that best fit their specific circumstances. In addition, they help increase nonprofits' capacity to monitor themselves.

TIP

No law requires bylaws or policies to be written in "legalese." Use clear language to make your statements understandable without ambiguity so they are not open to many different interpretations.

NONPROFIT GOVERNANCE PRINCIPLES

The Panel on the Nonprofit Sector, convened by Independent Sector — a leadership forum for charities, foundations, and corporate giving programs committed to advancing the common good in America and around the world — issued its principles for good governance for public and private charitable organizations. The principles are predicated on the need for a "careful balance between the two essential forms of regulation

— that is, between prudent legal mandates to ensure that organizations do not abuse the privilege of their exempt status, and, for all other aspects of sound operations, well-informed self-governance and mutual awareness among nonprofit organizations."

These 33 principles, organized under four categories, are as follows (slightly edited for brevity):

Legal Compliance and Public Disclosure

1. An organization must comply with applicable federal, state, and local law. If the organization conducts programs outside the United States, it must abide by applicable international laws and conventions that are legally binding on the United States.

2. An organization should have a formally adopted, written code of ethics with which all of its directors, staff, and volunteers are familiar and to which they adhere.

3. An organization should implement policies and procedures to ensure that all conflicts of interest, or appearance of them, within the organization and its board are appropriately managed though disclosure, recusal, or other means.

4. An organization should implement policies and procedures that enable individuals to come forward with information on illegal practices or violations of organizational policies. This whistleblower policy should specify that the organization will not retaliate against, and will protect the confidentiality of, individuals who make good-faith reports.

5. An organization should implement policies and procedures to preserve the organization's important documents and business records.

6. An organization's board should ensure that the organization has adequate plans to protect its assets — its property, financial and human resources, programmatic content and material, and integrity and reputation — against damage or loss. The board should regularly review the organization's need for general liability and directors' and officers' liability insurance, as well as take other actions to mitigate risk.

7. An organization should make information about its operations, including its governance, finances, programs, and other activities, widely available to the public. Charitable organizations should also consider making information available on the methods they use to evaluate the outcomes of their work and sharing the results of the evaluations.

TIP

Develop an annual evaluation process to ensure the board provides the chief executive with formal feedback regarding on-the-job performance. According to BoardSource's *Governance Index 2007,* chief executives who receive a written evaluation are more satisfied with their jobs than those who don't — 88 percent versus 78 percent.

EFFECTIVE GOVERNANCE

8. An organization must have a governing body that is responsible for approving the organization's mission and strategic direction, annual budget, key financial transactions, compensation practices, and fiscal and governance policies.

9. The board of an organization should meet regularly to conduct its business and fulfill its duties.

10. The board of an organization should establish and periodically review its size and structure. The board should have enough members to allow for full deliberation and diversity of thinking on organizational matters. Except for very small organizations, this generally means that a board should have at least five members.

11. The board of an organization should include members with the diverse background (including ethnic, racial, and gender perspectives), experience, and organizational and financial skills necessary to advance the organization's mission.

12. A substantial majority of the board (usually at least two-thirds) of a public charity should be independent.

Independent members should not be compensated by the organization as employees or independent contractors, have their compensation determined by individuals who are compensated by the organization, receive material financial benefits from the organization except as a member of a charitable class served by the organization, or be related to or reside with any person described above.

13. The board should hire, oversee, and annually evaluate the performance of the organization's chief executive. It should conduct such an evaluation prior to any change in the chief executive's compensation, unless a multiyear contract is in force or the change consists solely of routine adjustments for inflation or cost of living.

14. The board of an organization that has paid staff should ensure that separate individuals hold the positions of chief staff officer, board chair, and board treasurer. Organizations without paid staff should ensure that the positions of board chair and treasurer are separately held.

15. The board should establish an effective, systematic process for educating and communicating with board members to ensure that they are aware of their legal and ethical responsibilities, are knowledgeable about the programs and other activities of the organization, and can effectively carry out their oversight functions.

16. Board members should evaluate their performance as a group and as individuals at least every three years. The board should have clear procedures for removing members who are unable to fulfill their responsibilities.

17. The board should establish clear policies and procedures setting the length of terms and the number of consecutive terms a board member may serve.

18. The board should review the organization's governing instruments at least every five years.

19. The board should regularly review the organization's mission and goals and evaluate at least every five years the organization's goals, programs, and other activities to be sure they advance its mission and make prudent use of its resources.

20. Board members are generally expected to serve without compensation, other than reimbursement for expenses incurred to fulfill their board duties. An organization that provides compensation to its board members should use appropriate comparability data to determine the amount to be paid; document the decision; and provide full disclosure to anyone, on request, of the amount and rationale for the compensation.

STRONG FINANCIAL OVERSIGHT

21. An organization must keep complete, current, and accurate financial records. Its board should review timely reports of the organization's financial activities and have a qualified, independent financial expert audit or review these statements annually in a manner appropriate to the organization's size and scale of operations.

22. The board of an organization must institute policies and procedures to ensure that the organization (and, if applicable, its subsidiaries) manages and invests its funds responsibly, in accordance with requirements of law. The full board should approve the organization's annual budget and monitor performance against the budget.

23. An organization should not provide loans (or the equivalent, such as guaranteeing loans, purchasing or transferring ownership of a residence or office, or relieving a debt or lease obligations) to its directors or officers.

24. An organization should spend a significant portion of its annual budget on programs that pursue its mission. The budget should provide sufficient resources for effective administration of the organization and, if it solicits contributions, for appropriate fundraising activities.

25. An organization should establish clear, written policies for paying or reimbursing expenses incurred by anyone conducting business or traveling on its behalf, including the types of expenses that can be paid or reimbursed and the documentation required. These policies should require that travel on behalf of the organization is to be undertaken in a cost-effective manner.

26. An organization should neither pay for nor reimburse travel expenditures for spouses, dependents, or others who are accompanying someone conducting business for the organization unless they are also conducting the business.

PITFALL

Providing loans to senior executives as a benefit of employment will not only attract the attention of the IRS but could lead to financial penalties known as intermediate sanctions if the IRS determines the executives received an excess benefit.

RESPONSIBLE FUNDRAISING

27. Solicitation materials and other communications addressed to prospective donors and the public must clearly identify the organization and be accurate and truthful.

28. Contributions must be used for purposes consistent with the donor's intent, whether as described in the solicitation materials or as directed by the donor.

29. Donors must receive acknowledgments of their charitable contributions to an organization, in accordance with federal tax law requirements, including information to facilitate the donor's compliance with tax law requirements.

30. An organization should adopt clear policies to determine whether acceptance of a gift would compromise its ethics, financial circumstances, program focus, or other interests.

31. An organization should provide appropriate training and supervision of the people soliciting funds on its behalf to ensure that they understand their responsibilities and applicable law and do not employ techniques that are coercive, intimidating, or intended to harass potential donors.

32. An organization should not compensate internal or external fundraisers on the basis of a commission or percentage of the amount raised.

33. An organization should respect the privacy of individual donors and, except where disclosure is required by law, should not sell or otherwise make available the names and contact information of its donors without providing them an opportunity to at least annually opt out of use of their names.

ANNUAL INFORMATION RETURN

Most tax-exempt organizations must file an annual information form (Form 990) with the IRS. This enables the IRS to ensure that these organizations continue to meet the requirements for their tax-exempt status. At the same time, all the data collected through these forms help the entire nonprofit sector monitor growth and trends, track the types of needs being addressed by nonprofits, and identify specific practices adopted by nonprofit organizations.

CHIEF EXECUTIVE COMPENSATION

One of the board's toughest tasks is to determine appropriate compensation for the chief executive. The board should keep in mind the following issues as it determines the appropriate benefit package for the chief executive:

Compliance

- Focus on reasonableness. Excessive benefits raise a red flag.

- Be familiar with the intermediate sanctions rules to avoid potentially heavy penalties. These rules, which are primarily applicable to public charities, impose excise taxes on board members and other insiders for engaging in excess benefit transactions, including payment of excessive compensation. (More information about these rules is in the glossary.)

- Follow the intermediate sanctions safe harbor procedures: Rely on comparative studies to give direction; record your process for making the decision; and have an independent board approve the benefit package. (These procedures are also collectively known as the rebuttable presumption of reasonableness.)

Compensation philosophy

- Your organizational compensation philosophy understands the battery of issues that impact the organization's capacity and willingness to remunerate employees for good work done. It takes into account internal and external challenges, compliance requirements, financial means, and numerous value-based standards influencing the culture within the organization.

Relevance

- Consider the expectations for the position, budget and staff size of the organization, scope and location of the organization, and experience of the chief executive.

Performance

- Review the compensation package annually after performance evaluation. Tie compensation to performance. It is acceptable to provide bonuses and incentive pay as long as they are not percentage based.

Reporting

- Remember that compensation needs to be reported on your Form 990. It is public knowledge.

- On your Form 990, separate accurately the base salary, bonuses, and deferred compensation.

- Make sure the full board is familiar with the full package (including potential severance clauses) and reviews the Form 990 before filing.

The IRS substantially revised the Form 990 in 2008. Previously, information collected via the Form 990 had focused on financial data (revenue and expenses). Now, this annual return seeks extensive information in the form of facts, with answers in prose, not numbers; organizations need to report on fundraising, gaming, international programs, non-cash receipts, joint ventures, use of subsidiaries, and much more. With the form's revision, the IRS introduced a segment on governance that poses numerous questions related to specific board structures and practices. Indeed, this return is intended to influence and modify nonprofit organizations' behavior by encouraging their governing boards to adopt certain policies and procedures (so they can check "yes" rather than "no" boxes).

The federal tax law requires almost none of these policies and procedures. Still, a nonprofit organization filing Form 990 is required to report

- the total number of voting members of its governing body and the number of these members who are independent

- whether a trustee, director, officer, or key employee has a family relationship or a business relationship with any other trustee, director, officer, or key employee

- whether control over management duties customarily performed by or under the direct supervision of trustees, directors, officers, or key employees has been delegated to a management company or other person

- whether a copy of the annual information return was provided to each member of its governing body before being filed

- whether contemporaneous documentation is in place for meetings of the governing body, committee meetings (if the committee has authority to act on behalf of the governing body), and for decisions and actions undertaken by the governing body

- whether and, if so, how the governing documents, conflict-of-interest policy, and financial statements are available to the public

TIP

Posting your Form 990 on your Web site or at www.guidestar.org provides your organization with an excellent opportunity to market itself and highlight its accomplishments to potential supporters, clients, or members.

In the past, board members demonstrated adherence to their duties and responsibilities largely by action, rather than by documentation. The only documentation of any substance was properly prepared minutes. Today, however, a nonprofit board is expected to not only function appropriately but also be able to prove it.

The IRS expects the annual information return to address good practices, in the form of written policies or procedures that nonprofit, tax-exempt organizations have adopted. In particular, the form asks the filing organization to report or describe whether it has

1. A conflict-of-interest policy (see Chapter 1 and the Appendix)

2. A whistleblower policy (see the Appendix)

3. A document retention and destruction policy (see the Appendix)

4. Policies and procedures governing the activities of any chapters, branches, or affiliates, to ensure that their operations are consistent with those of the organization

5. Invested in, contributed assets to, or participated in a joint venture or similar arrangement with a taxable entity during the year. (If the answer to this question is yes, the organization must report whether it has adopted a written policy or procedure requiring it to evaluate its participation in joint venture arrangements under the federal tax law and has taken steps to safeguard its exempt status with respect to these arrangements.)

6. A process for determining compensation of its chief executive officer, executive director, top management official, and/or other officers or key employees that includes a review and approval by independent persons, comparability data, and contemporaneous substantiation of the deliberation and decision

7. A policy regarding the periodic monitoring, inspection, and enforcement of any conservation easements it holds

8. Procedures for monitoring use of grant funds, if it makes grants to recipients outside the United States

9. A charity care policy (only if functioning as a hospital)

10. A debt collection policy (only if functioning as a hospital)

11. A policy regarding payment or reimbursement of expenses incurred by directors, officers, and key employees regarding first-class or charter travel, travel for companions, tax indemnification and gross-up payments, a discretionary spending account, a housing allowance or residence for personal use, payments for business use of a personal residence, health or social club dues or initiation fees, and/or personal services (such as for a maid, chauffeur, or chef)

12. A gift acceptance policy (for so-called nonstandard gifts)

13. A mission statement approved and periodically reviewed by the board

Also, although not required by this annual return, some charitable organizations have policies concerning the use of volunteers, including the execution of confidentiality agreements.

A nonprofit board that institutes and adheres to appropriate policies and procedures, and has individual members who understand their legal duties and responsibilities, is likely to be strong and effective. That, however, is not enough. On behalf of the organization, board members must also ensure that compliance, vigilance, and transparency are part of ongoing operations.

QUESTIONS THE BOARD SHOULD ASK

1. How well does our organization perform against the nonprofit governance principles articulated by the Panel on the Nonprofit Sector?

2. Has every board member reviewed the organization's IRS Form 990 or other annual information return (preferably, before it is filed)?

3. Did we receive a clean audit? Have we addressed all the issues mentioned in the auditor's management letter?

4. Do we adhere to safe harbor processes (the rebuttable presumption under the intermediate sanctions rules [see the glossary], when we determine the chief executive's compensation? Who on the board is responsible for that?

5. Have we developed all of the written policies or procedures referenced on Form 990 that are appropriate for our organization?

CONCLUSION

TOWARD A BETTER BOARD

In the wake of the collapse of and major damage to large corporations and accounting firms in the early 2000s, regulators, legislators, watchdog groups, and the media heightened their focus on matters of corporate governance. Statutory law was enacted, followed by sweeping rules and regulations. Litigation on the subject is widespread. The IRS has launched a massive effort to promulgate and impose numerous governance standards on public charities. Although most of this legislation does not currently apply to nonprofit organizations, that situation can always change.

As a result, every board must understand the framework within which its organization functions — which laws and regulations must be respected and how it can carry out its duties to meet all organizational, collective, and individual legal obligations. These responsibilities are grouped into three areas of vigilance for nonprofit boards and board members: mission, oversight, and personal action. By using this chapter as a checklist, a nonprofit board can help protect the organization, the board, and its members from liability.

THREE THINGS TO REMEMBER

1. BE A GUARDIAN OF THE MISSION.

Every organization needs to define its fundamental purpose, philosophy, and values, and find appropriate ways to tie them into meaningful activities. Without a purpose and mission, an organization has no mandate. The primary role and most important duty of the board is to act as the guardian of that mission.

_____ **Fully understand and be able to articulate the organization's mission at any given time.** By drafting a clear and concise mission statement, the board has a tool for judging the success of the organization and its programs. This statement helps to verify whether the board is on the right track and making the correct decisions. It provides direction when the organization needs to adapt to new demands. Attention to mission helps the board adhere to its primary purpose and resolve conflicts during decision making. (For more on mission, see *The Nonprofit Board's Role in Mission, Planning, and Evaluation,* Book 5 in the BoardSource Governance Series.)

_____ **Understand the overall operations of the organization.** Board members need to be familiar with the programs and services that carry out the organization's mandate. They also need to understand the various business activities the organization undertakes, such as fundraising, lobbying, and unrelated business, to ensure that the activities are appropriate for the organization and do not jeopardize its tax-exempt status. (See the glossary for legal definitions of these terms.)

_____ **Read and understand materials prepared and distributed by the organization.** These include annual reports, promotional materials, publications, catalogs, newsletters, and fundraising brochures. This exercise not only helps the board ensure that the organization is represented accurately to the public but also familiarizes board members with the organization's programs and services.

2. ENSURE COMPLIANCE WITH LAWS AND RULES.

Most nonprofit organizations function within the legal framework created by the federal government and state where they carry on business. An organization must also operate according to its own formal documents and the commitments it has made to various stakeholders. If the board is not familiar with and sensitive to the applicable laws, rules, and guidelines, it becomes vulnerable to liability and jeopardizes the organization's legal status.

_____ **Understand the organization's form — whether it is a corporation, unincorporated association, or a trust.** Board members should also know what is required to maintain that form and see to it that the necessary action is taken to respect that form (see Chapter 2).

_____ **Feel comfortable about the IRS regulations affecting the tax-exempt status of the organization.** The IRS does not grant the status (Congress does) but recognizes it if appropriate forms are filed correctly and the organization continues to meet the appropriate legal requirements.

_____ **Periodically review the bylaws to ensure that the organization is in compliance with its governing documents.** On top of the hierarchy of laws that govern nonprofit corporations sit the federal and state corporate and tax laws. Articles of incorporation clarify the main features of the organization; they are broader and less flexible than bylaws. Bylaws, in turn, articulate the corporate structure in more detail and outline the fundamental governance processes. They set the rules, which, when followed, help provide legal protection to the board members. Additional policies and resolutions provide even more specific guidelines for board and staff action.

_____ **Know the jurisdictions in which the organization does business.** While it sounds as though it applies only to commercial enterprises, "doing business" also applies to nonprofits. In addition to the state where the main office is located, a nonprofit organization may also do business in other jurisdictions. If this is the case, the board should be advised of those locations and ensure that appropriate registrations and reporting take place.

_____ **Understand the relationship between and among the organization's related entities and assess their purpose.** For example, a membership association may have a related foundation, a political action committee, or a for-profit subsidiary. A charitable organization may have a separate organization that functions as a lobbying arm, or an advocacy organization may have a separate educational foundation. These organizations are likely to have different tax-exempt statuses. When an organization and a related entity have overlapping boards, officers, and/or employees, exercise caution to avoid having the activities of one entity attributed to the other for federal tax purposes (such as extensive legislative activities of a lobbying entity attributed to a public charity).

_____ **Engage an auditor to attest to the reliability of the organization's financial condition.** Except in the case of federally funded programs, no federal law requires a nonprofit to have an annual independent audit. Only one state has such a requirement (known as the California Nonprofit Integrity Act). Still, by commissioning an audit, the board provides an added incentive for proper resource management and helps produce a tool to encourage open communication with stakeholders. Small nonprofits with a simple and straightforward financial structure — and limited resources — can rely on reviews or even compilation of financial statements by a certified public accountant. (For more information on audits, see *Financial Responsibilities of Nonprofit Boards,* Book 3 in the BoardSource Governance Series.)

_____ **Safeguard the tax-exempt status of the organization.** The board must ensure that the organization withholds employee income taxes, respects employment-related laws, and files Form 990 and necessary state forms accurately and on time. If the board is not vigilant about these practices, the government may impose serious financial penalties and excise taxes on individual board members and possibly revoke the organization's tax-exempt status. Also, the board must be aware of and follow all safe harbor measures when overseeing any financial contracts or compensation.

3. PROMOTE COLLECTIVE AND INDIVIDUAL VIGILANCE.
One approach a nonprofit board can take to guard against legal liability is to focus on actions individual board members can take. Here are some practical ideas and processes to help board members become more organized, more knowledgeable, and more cautious about fulfilling their duties.

_____ **Have an up-to-date board book.** It need not be particularly formal or fancy; a simple three-ring binder will suffice. The book should include, at a minimum, the following documents: a board roster and address (including e-mail) list, the organization's articles, bylaws, IRS determination letter, other documents with legal overtones, recent board meeting minutes, a copy of the most recently filed Form 990, and the latest financial statements. In addition, a board book should include job descriptions for the board and a list of expectations for individual board members.

_____ **Keep up with issues that affect the functioning and future of the organization.** Consider organizing periodic board retreats and attending occasional educational seminars. Such experiences can help place the nonprofit organization's activities in perspective and help board members more fully understand the board's structure, operations, and responsibilities. Continuous board education, starting with comprehensive orientation, is one of the most effective ways to provide the members of the board with incentive and requisite tools to do their job conscientiously. In fact, 93 percent of board members who responded to BoardSource's *Nonprofit Governance Index 2007* survey express interest in receiving additional governance training and information.

_____ **Regularly attend board meetings.** Obviously, schedule conflicts will arise at times; if the board member cannot attend a meeting, the minutes should reflect that fact and why. A board member cannot exercise the requisite degree of fiduciary responsibility without attending meetings and interacting with the other members.

_____ **Actively participate in the decision-making process.** Silence is deemed to be concurrence. Board members who oppose an action to be undertaken by the organization at the behest of the board should speak up and be certain the minutes note their dissent.

_____ **Ask questions.** Whether in the boardroom or outside of a meeting, failure to ask questions is one of the worst nonactions of a board member. Board members who merely pretend to understand what is happening only fool themselves — and place themselves in a position to cause harm to the organization or themselves. Questions may be asked of other board members, the organization's officers, staff, lawyers, and other professionals. Questions may be posed during the course of a board meeting or on other occasions.

____ **Give careful consideration to board minutes.** There should be minutes of every board meeting, prepared with a heavy dose of common sense and perspective. These are not verbatim transcripts of the proceedings but summaries of important actions taken during the meeting. A good test of the format is whether someone, years later, is able to grasp the essence of what took place at the meeting and the nature of the decisions made.

When subject to legal action, organizations often must produce their minutes. Consequently, minutes should be written with an expectation that someday the document could serve as an exhibit in a court case. A corollary to this is that board members should carefully read draft meeting minutes before approving them.

____ **Stay within bounds.** When acting in its volunteer capacity, the board should not exceed its proper authority. The members of the board serve as overseers, not day-to-day managers. Their role is to make extraordinary, not ordinary, strategic decisions. The board should oversee the programs of the organization — not meddle in tasks that it has delegated to the chief executive.

How this works in practice will vary considerably. If the organization has a chief executive, that person will provide most of the information the board needs. (Still, questions should be asked.) Some boards prefer to meet only when the organization's chief executive is present. Others reserve time to meet in an executive session, without the chief executive or other staff present. The chief executive may be an ex officio but nonvoting member of the board or may be a voting member. In the latter case, the chief executive may recuse himself to facilitate an executive session.

As a collective body, the board ensures that the organization functions within the framework of and in advancement of its mission, makes sure that the organization's resources are adequate and appropriately protected, and provides sufficient oversight. Whether or not accountable to another body, such as a membership or a parent organization, a board is *always* accountable to the public trust.

When a board neglects its legal and moral obligations, the entire sector suffers because the public trust in nonprofit organizations is weakened. On the other hand, board members who carry out the tasks assigned to them, come to meetings regularly and fully prepared, make independent and unbiased decisions, and disclose any conflicts of interest help advance the nonprofit sector as a whole and the organization they serve in particular.

Board member service should be a richly rewarding experience — and it will be for a board that diligently educates itself on its individual and collective legal duties and responsibilities.

APPENDIX
SAMPLE POLICIES

The following sample policies are excerpted from The Nonprofit Policy Sampler, Second Edition, *by Barbara Lawrence and Outi Flynn (BoardSource, 2006). Nonprofit organizations that find the following samples helpful may adapt the documents to their own structure.*

SAMPLE CODE OF ETHICAL CONDUCT

I. Personal and Professional Integrity
All staff, board members, and volunteers of XYZ act with honesty, integrity, and openness in all their dealings as representatives of the organization. The organization promotes a working environment that values respect, fairness, and integrity.

II. Mission
XYZ has a clearly stated mission and purpose, approved by the board, in pursuit of the public good. All of its programs support that mission and all who work for or on behalf of the organization understand and are loyal to that mission and purpose.

III. Governance
XYZ has an active governing body, the board, which is responsible for setting the mission and strategic direction of the organization and oversight of the finances, operations, and policies of XYZ. The board

- ensures that its members have the requisite skills and experience to carry out their duties and that all members understand and fulfill their governance duties acting for the benefit of XYZ and its public purpose

- has a conflict-of-interest policy that ensures that any conflicts of interest or the appearance thereof are avoided or appropriately managed through disclosure, recusal, or other means

- has a statement of personal commitment that attests to the commitment to XYZ's goals and values

- is responsible for the hiring, firing, and regular review of the performance of its chief executive, and ensures that the compensation of the chief executive, the chief financial officer, and other senior management positions as the board deems appropriate

- ensures that the chief executive and appropriate staff provide the board with timely and comprehensive information so that the board can effectively carry out its duties

- ensures that XYZ conducts all transactions and dealings with integrity and honesty

- ensures that XYZ promotes working relationships with board members, staff, volunteers, and program beneficiaries that are based on mutual respect, fairness, and openness

- ensures that the organization is fair and inclusive in its hiring and promotion policies and practices for all board, staff, and volunteer positions

- ensures that policies of XYZ are in writing, clearly articulated, and officially adopted

- is responsible for engaging independent auditors to perform an annual audit of XYZ's financial statements, and has an audit committee that is responsible for overseeing the reliability of financial reporting (usually the responsibility of the finance committee), including the effectiveness of internal control over financial reporting, reviewing, and discussing the annual audited financial statements to determine whether they are complete and consistent with operational and other information known to the committee members, understanding significant risks and exposures and management's response to minimize the risks, and understanding the audit scope and approving audit and non–audit services

- ensures that the resources of XYZ are responsibly and prudently managed

- ensures that XYZ has the capacity to carry out its programs effectively

IV. Responsible Stewardship

XYZ manages its funds responsibly and prudently. This should include the following considerations:

- spends an adequate amount on administrative expenses to ensure effective accounting systems, internal controls, competent staff, and other expenditures critical to professional management

- compensates staff, and any others who may receive compensation, reasonably and appropriately

- knows that solicitation of funds has reasonable fundraising costs, recognizing the variety of factors that affect fundraising costs

- does not accumulate operating funds excessively

- draws prudently from endowment funds consistent with donor intent and to support the public purpose of XYZ

- ensures that all spending practices and policies are fair, reasonable, and appropriate to fulfill the mission of XYZ

- ensures that all financial reports are factually accurate and complete in all material respects

V. Openness and Disclosure

XYZ provides comprehensive and timely information to the public, the media, and all stakeholders and is responsive in a timely manner to reasonable requests for information. All information about XYZ will fully and honestly reflect the policies and practices of the organization. Basic informational data about XYZ, such as the Form 990, will be posted online or otherwise made available to the public. All solicitation materials accurately represent XYZ's policies and practices and will reflect the dignity of program beneficiaries. All financial, organizational, and program reports will be complete and accurate in all material respects.

VI. Legal Compliance

XYZ is knowledgeable of, and complies with, laws and regulations.

VII. Program Evaluation

XYZ regularly reviews program effectiveness and has mechanisms to incorporate lessons learned into future programs. The organization is committed to improving program and organizational effectiveness and develops mechanisms to promote learning from its activities and the field. XYZ is responsive to changes in its field of activity and is responsive to the needs of its constituencies.

VIII. Inclusiveness and Diversity

XYZ has a policy of promoting inclusiveness and its staff, board, and volunteers reflect diversity in order to enrich its programmatic effectiveness. XYZ takes meaningful steps to promote inclusiveness in its hiring, retention, promotion, board recruitment, and constituencies served.

IX. Fundraising

XYZ solicitation of funds from the public or from donor institutions uses material that is truthful about the organization. XYZ respects the privacy concerns of individual donors and expends funds consistent with donor intent. XYZ discloses important and relevant information to potential donors.

In raising funds from the public, XYZ will respect the rights of donors, as follows:

Donors will be informed of the mission of XYZ, the way the resources will be used, and their capacity to use donations effectively for their intended purpose. Further, they will

- be informed of the identity of those serving on XYZ's governing board and to expect the board to exercise prudent judgment in its stewardship responsibilities

- have access to XYZ's most recent financial reports

- be assured their gifts will be used for purposes for which they are given

- receive appropriate acknowledgment and recognition

- be assured that information about their donations is handled with respect and with confidentiality to the extent provided by law

- be approached in a professional manner

- be informed whether those seeking donations are volunteers, employees of XYZ, or hired solicitors

- have the opportunity for their names to be deleted from mailing lists that XYZ may intend to share

- be encouraged to ask questions when making a donation and to receive prompt, truthful, and forthright answers

REPORTING RESPONSIBILITY

It is the responsibility of all directors, officers, and employees to comply with the code of ethical conduct and to report violations or suspected violations to the compliance officer (secretary/treasurer) in accordance with the whistleblower policy. The compliance officer will notify the sender and acknowledge receipt of the reported violation or suspected violation within five business days, unless the submission of the violation is anonymous. All reports will be promptly investigated and appropriate corrective action will be taken if warranted by the investigation.

SAMPLE CONFLICT-OF-INTEREST STATEMENT

REASON FOR STATEMENT

XYZ, as a nonprofit, tax-exempt organization, depends on charitable contributions from the public. Maintenance of its tax-exempt status is important both for its continued financial stability and for the receipt of contributions and public support. Therefore, the operations of XYZ first must fulfill all legal requirements. They also depend on the public trust and thus are subject to scrutiny by and accountability to both governmental authorities and members of the public.

Consequently, there exists between XYZ and its board, officers, and management employees a fiduciary duty that carries with it a broad and unbending duty of loyalty and fidelity. The board, officers, and management employees have the responsibility of administering the affairs of XYZ honestly and prudently, and of exercising their best care, skill, and judgment for the sole benefit of XYZ. Those persons shall exercise the utmost good faith in all transactions involved in their duties, and they shall not use their positions with XYZ or knowledge gained therefrom for their personal benefit. The interests of the organization must have the first priority in all decisions and actions.

PERSONS CONCERNED

This statement is directed not only to board members and officers, but to all employees who can influence the actions of XYZ. For example, this includes all who make purchasing decisions, all other persons who might be described as "management personnel," and all who have proprietary information concerning XYZ.

KEY AREAS IN WHICH CONFLICT MAY ARISE

Conflicts of interest may arise in the relations of directors, officers, and management employees with any of the following third parties:

- persons and firms supplying goods and services to XYZ

- persons and firms from whom XYZ leases property and equipment

- persons and firms with whom XYZ is dealing or planning to deal in connection with the gift, purchase or sale of real estate, securities, or other property

- competing or affinity organizations

- donors and others supporting XYZ

- recipients of grants from XYZ

- agencies, organizations, and associations that affect the operations of XYZ

- family members, friends, and other employees

Nature of Conflicting Interest

A material conflicting interest may be defined as an interest, direct or indirect, with any persons and firms mentioned in Section [ABC]. Such an interest might arise, for example, through

1. Owning stock or holding debt or other proprietary interests in any third party dealing with XYZ

2. Holding office, serving on the board, participating in management, or being otherwise employed (or formerly employed) by any third party dealing with XYZ

3. Receiving remuneration for services with respect to individual transactions involving XYZ

4. Using XYZ's time, personnel, equipment, supplies, or good will other than for approved XYZ activities, programs, and purposes

5. Receiving personal gifts or loans from third parties dealing with XYZ. Receipt of any gift is disapproved except gifts of nominal value that could not be refused without discourtesy. No personal gift of money should ever be accepted.

Interpretation of This Statement of Policy

The areas of conflicting interest listed in Section [ABC], and the relations in those areas that may give rise to conflict, as listed in Section [DEF], are not exhaustive. Conceivably, conflicts might arise in other areas or through other relations. It is assumed that the trustees, officers, and management employees will recognize such areas and relation by analogy.

The fact that one of the interests described in Section [DEF] exists does not mean necessarily that a conflict exists, or that the conflict, if it exists, is material enough to be of practical importance, or if material, that upon full disclosure of all relevant facts and circumstances, that it is necessarily adverse to the interests of XYZ.

However, it is the policy of the board that the existence of any of the interests described in Section [DEF] shall be disclosed on a timely basis and always before any transaction is consummated. It shall be the continuing responsibility of board, officers, and management employees to scrutinize their transactions and outside business interests and relationships for potential conflicts and to immediately make such disclosures.

DISCLOSURE POLICY AND PROCEDURE

Disclosure should be made according to XYZ standards. Transactions with related parties may be undertaken only if all of the following are observed:

1. A material transaction is fully disclosed in the audited financial statements of the organization;

2. The related party is excluded from the discussion and approval of such transaction;

3. A competitive bid or comparable valuation exists; and

4. The organization's board has acted upon and demonstrated that the transaction is in the best interest of the organization.

Staff disclosures should be made to the chief executive (or if he or she is the one with the conflict, then to the designated committee), who shall determine whether a conflict exists and is material, and if the matters are material, bring them to the attention of the designated committee.

Disclosure involving directors should be made to the designated committee.

The board shall determine whether a conflict exists and is material, and in the presence of an existing material conflict, whether the contemplated transaction may be authorized as just, fair, and reasonable to XYZ. The decision of the board on these matters will rest in their sole discretion, and their concern must be the welfare of XYZ and the advancement of its purpose.

SAMPLE WHISTLEBLOWER PROTECTION POLICY

This policy provides clear definitions and provisions for handling allegations of misconduct while protecting the organization under difficult circumstances.

In keeping with the policy of maintaining the highest standards of conduct and ethics, XYZ will investigate any suspected fraudulent or dishonest use or misuse of XYZ's resources or property by staff, board members, consultants, or volunteers.

Staff, board members, consultants, and volunteers are encouraged to report suspected fraudulent or dishonest conduct (i.e., to act as "whistleblower"), pursuant to the procedures set forth below.

REPORTING

A person's concerns about possible fraudulent or dishonest use or misuse of resources or property should be reported to his or her supervisor or, if suspected by a volunteer, to the staff member supporting the volunteer's work. If, for any reason, a person finds it difficult to report his or her concerns to a supervisor or staff member supporting the volunteer's work, the person may report the concerns directly to the chief executive. Alternately, to facilitate reporting of suspected violations where the reporter wishes to remain anonymous, a written statement may be submitted to one of the individuals listed above.

DEFINITIONS

Baseless Allegations

Allegations made with reckless disregard for their truth or falsity. Individuals making such allegations may be subject to disciplinary action by XYZ, and/or legal claims by individuals accused of such conduct.

Fraudulent or Dishonest Conduct

A deliberate act or failure to act with the intention of obtaining an unauthorized benefit. Examples of such conduct include

- forgery or alteration of documents

- unauthorized alteration or manipulation of computer files

- fraudulent financial reporting

- pursuit of a benefit or advantage in violation of XYZ's Conflict-of-Interest Policy

- misappropriation or misuse of XYZ resources, such as funds, supplies, or other assets

- authorizing or receiving compensation for goods not received or services not performed

- authorizing or receiving compensation for hours not worked

Whistleblower

An employee, consultant, or volunteer who informs a supervisor or the chief executive about an activity relating to XYZ which that person believes to be fraudulent or dishonest.

RIGHTS AND RESPONSIBILITIES

Supervisors

Supervisors are required to report suspected fraudulent or dishonest conduct to the chief executive. Reasonable care should be taken in dealing with suspected misconduct to avoid

- baseless allegations

- premature notice to persons suspected of misconduct and/or disclosure of suspected misconduct to others not involved with the investigation

- violations of a person's rights under law

Due to the important yet sensitive nature of the suspected violations, effective professional follow-up is critical. Supervisors, while appropriately concerned about "getting to the bottom" of such issues, should not in any circumstances perform any investigative or other follow-up steps on their own. Accordingly, a supervisor who becomes aware of suspected misconduct

- should not contact the person suspected to further investigate the matter or demand restitution

- should not discuss the case with attorneys, the media, or anyone other than the chief executive

- should not report the case to an authorized law enforcement officer without first discussing the case with the chief executive

Investigation

All relevant matters, including suspected but unproved matters, will be reviewed and analyzed, with documentation of the receipt, retention, investigation, and treatment of the complaint. Appropriate corrective action will be taken, if necessary, and findings will be communicated to the reporting person and his or her supervisor. Investigations may warrant investigation by independent persons such as auditors and/or attorneys.

Whistleblower Protection

XYZ will protect whistleblowers as defined below:

- XYZ will use its best efforts to protect whistleblowers against retaliation. Whistleblowing complaints will be handled with sensitivity, discretion, and confidentiality to the extent allowed by the circumstances and the law. Generally, this means that whistleblower complaints will only be shared with those who have a need to know so that XYZ can conduct an effective investigation, determine what action to take based on the results of any such investigation, and in appropriate cases, with law enforcement personnel. (Should disciplinary or legal action be taken against a person or persons as a result of a whistleblower complaint, such persons may also have the right to know the identity of the whistleblower.)

- Employees, consultants, and volunteers of XYZ may not retaliate against a whistleblower for informing management about an activity which that person believes to be fraudulent or dishonest with the intent or effect of adversely affecting the terms or conditions of the whistleblower's employment, including but not limited to, threats of physical harm, loss of job, punitive work assignments, or impact on salary or fees. Whistleblowers who believe that they have been retaliated against may file a written complaint with the chief executive. Any complaint of retaliation will be promptly investigated and appropriate corrective measures taken if allegations of retaliation are substantiated. This protection from retaliation is not intended to prohibit supervisors from taking action, including disciplinary action, in the usual scope of their duties and based on valid performance-related factors.

- Whistleblowers must be cautious to avoid baseless allegations (as described earlier in the definitions section of this policy).

SAMPLE DOCUMENT RETENTION AND DESTRUCTION POLICY

PURPOSE

In accordance with the Sarbanes-Oxley Act, which makes it a crime to alter, cover up, falsify, or destroy any document with the intent of impeding or obstructing any official proceeding, this policy provides for the systematic review, retention, and destruction of documents received or created by XYZ in connection with the transaction of organization business.

This policy covers all records and documents, regardless of physical form, contains guidelines for how long certain documents should be kept, and how records should be destroyed (unless under a legal hold). The policy is designed to ensure compliance with federal and state laws and regulations, to eliminate accidental or innocent destruction of records, and to facilitate XYZ's operations by promoting efficiency and freeing up valuable storage space.

DOCUMENT RETENTION

XYZ follows the document retention procedures outlined below. Documents that are not listed, but are substantially similar to those listed in the schedule, will be retained for the appropriate length of time.

Corporate Records

Annual Reports to Secretary of State Attorney General	Permanent
Articles of Incorporation	Permanent
Board Meeting and Board Committee Minutes	Permanent
Board Policies/Resolutions	Permanent
Bylaws	Permanent
Construction Documents	Permanent
Fixed Asset Records	Permanent
IRS Application for Tax-Exempt Status (Form 1023)	Permanent
IRS Determination Letter	Permanent
State Sales Tax Exemption Letter	Permanent
Contracts (after expiration)	7 years
Correspondence (general)	3 years

Accounting and Corporate Tax Records

Annual Audits and Financial Statements	Permanent
Depreciation Schedules	Permanent
IRS Form 990 Tax Returns	Permanent
General Ledgers	Permanent
Business Expense Records	7 years
IRS Forms 1099	7 years
Journal Entries	7 years
Invoices	7 years
Sales Records (box office, concessions, gift shop)	5 years

Petty Cash Vouchers	3 years
Cash Receipts	3 years
Credit Card Receipts	3 years

Bank Records

Check Registers	[7 years/Permanent]
Bank Deposit Slips	7 years
Bank Statements and Reconciliation	7 years
Electronic Fund Transfer Documents	7 years

Payroll and Employment Tax Records

Payroll Registers	Permanent
State Unemployment Tax Records	Permanent
Earnings Records	7 years
Garnishment Records	7 years
Payroll Tax Returns	7 years
W-2 Statements	7 years

Employee Records

Employment and Termination Agreements	Permanent
Retirement and Pension Plan Documents	Permanent
Records Relating to Promotion, Demotion, or Discharge	7 years after termination
Accident Reports and Workers' Compensation Records	5 years
Salary Schedules	5 years
Employment Applications	3 years
I-9 Forms	3 years after termination
Time Cards	2 years

Donor and Grant Records

Donor Records and Acknowledgment Letters	7 years
Grant Applications and Contracts	7 years after completion

Legal, Insurance, and Safety Records

Appraisals	Permanent
Copyright Registrations	Permanent
Environmental Studies	Permanent
Insurance Policies	Permanent
Real Estate Documents	Permanent
Stock and Bond Records	Permanent
Trademark Registrations	Permanent
Leases	6 years after expiration
OSHA Documents	5 years
General Contracts	3 years after termination

ELECTRONIC DOCUMENTS AND RECORDS

Electronic documents will be retained as if they were paper documents. Therefore, any electronic files, including records of donations made online, that fall into one of the document types on the above schedule will be maintained for the appropriate amount of time. If a user has sufficient reason to keep an e-mail message, the message should be printed in hard copy and kept in the appropriate file or moved to an "archive" computer file folder. Backup and recovery methods will be tested on a regular basis.

EMERGENCY PLANNING

XYZ's records will be stored in a safe, secure, and accessible manner. Documents and financial files that are essential to keeping XYZ operating in an emergency will be duplicated or backed up at least every week and maintained off-site.

Document Destruction

XYZ's chief financial officer is responsible for the ongoing process of identifying its records, which have met the required retention period, and overseeing their destruction. Destruction of financial and personnel-related documents will be accomplished by shredding.

Document destruction will be suspended immediately, upon any indication of an official investigation or when a lawsuit is filed or appears imminent. Destruction will be reinstated upon conclusion of the investigation.

Compliance

Failure on the part of employees to follow this policy can result in possible civil and criminal sanctions against XYZ and its employees and possible disciplinary action against responsible individuals. The chief financial officer and finance committee chair will periodically review these procedures with legal counsel or the organization's certified public accountant to ensure that they are in compliance with new or revised regulations.

GLOSSARY

501(c)(3) charitable organizations — A 501(c)(3) nonprofit organization may be classified by the IRS as either a public charity (also called a public foundation) or a private foundation. Except for nonprofits that are automatically considered tax-exempt charities, such as churches, it is the organization's responsibility to notify the IRS, by filing Form 1023, that it wants to be a public charity or a private foundation. If it fails to qualify as a public charity, it will automatically be categorized as a private foundation. A public charity often is an institution or a publicly supported organization that provides services to the public.

Through the composition of its governing board and inclusive programs, an organization can become eligible for this tax-exempt status. The most common types of charitable organizations function as churches, colleges, universities, schools, health care institutions, arts institutions, or organizations that provide various services to the public. A private foundation can receive most of its resources from one source. It is the most suitable status for organizations that exist to distribute funding for charitable causes.

501(c)(4) social welfare organizations — Social welfare organizations are operated to advance the common good of the public and the welfare of the community in general. Advocacy often is their most effective action method; therefore, a key advantage of being qualified as a welfare organization is the ability to carry on unlimited lobbying. The major disadvantage is being unable to attract tax-deductible donations. Social welfare organizations file Form 1024 with the IRS to obtain recognition of their tax exemption.

501(c)(6) trade associations and professional societies — Business leagues and trade associations usually are formed to promote the common interest of people engaged in like businesses, or they are associations devoted to the improvement of business conditions of one or more lines of business as distinguished from the performance of particular services for individual persons. These organizations, which must advance the conditions of a particular trade or the interests of the community, can engage in unlimited lobbying. Donations are not tax deductible, but membership fees often can be deducted as a business expense. Trade associations file Form 1024 with the IRS to obtain recognition of their tax exemption.

Advocacy — Advocacy refers to the board member representing the organization in the community, articulating and speaking about the mission of the organization, and supporting and defending the organization's message or cause.

Annual information returns — With few exceptions, tax-exempt organizations must file an annual information return with the IRS. This is done by preparing Form 990 and sending it to the IRS by the 15th day of the fifth month after the end of the organization's accounting period (or pursuant to extension). On this form, the organization clarifies its mission and purpose and various governance practices, describes programmatic activities, reports revenue and expenses, and classifies income sources into taxable and nontaxable categories. Form 990 also is used to report the compensation levels of the highest-paid employees, current and former board members, and independent contractors. Indeed, Form 990 now requires the organization to report on just about all aspects of its operations — including governance practices.

Board of directors — Every nonprofit organization must have a board. Even if there is no staff, a board still must exist. The board is the responsible and liable body for the organization. It functions as the guardian of the mission and acts as the fiduciary — the trusted entity — for the resources. The board has three duties to the organization: care, loyalty, and obedience.

Charitable giving regulation — Not all nonprofit organizations are eligible to receive charitable contributions, nor are all contributions automatically and fully tax deductible. Federal tax law imposes a variety of rules (most related to record keeping and the value of the donation) that guide tax-exempt organizations when receiving and administering donations.

Charleston Principles — In 2001, the National Association of Attorneys General/National Association of State Charity Officials approved special guidelines addressing issues related to Internet fundraising. These principles serve as guidance to state officials to address the question of who has to register where.

Disclosure — Tax-exempt organizations are subject to many forms of disclosure. While transparency is the key to earning public trust, disclosure also allows the IRS to keep track of the activities of nonprofit organizations. The principal documents that tax-exempt organizations must make public include copies of their application for the tax-exempt status (IRS Form 1023 or 1024) and annual information returns (usually IRS Form 990) for the last three years. The organization must send a copy of these documents to anyone who asks; it may charge a reasonable (prepayment) photocopying fee, and specific rules apply in cases of harassment campaigns. If the organization posts its Form 990 on the Internet, it does not have to provide hard copies. The Form 990-T is also subject to this disclosure regime.

Excess benefit transaction — Financial exchanges between a tax-exempt organization and certain individuals are regulated by law. The most vulnerable transactions are chief executive compensation and any financial transactions carried out by the organization: paying for a vendor or consultant, rental or purchase agreements. Anything that exceeds fair market value or reasonable compensation for services rendered constitutes excessive benefit.

While the term "reasonable" is not well-defined by the federal tax law, an organization can protect itself if it abides by the following safe harbor (rebuttable presumption) rules: (1) rely on nationally recognized compensation and salary surveys for comparison; if these are not available, study similar organizations and their compensation for comparable positions; (2) document the rationale for the compensation, including the sources used to find comparative salary information; and (3) have an independent committee determine the compensation for the chief executive. When dealing with property, comparable prices and fair market value provide the guidelines for financial decisions. The organization may show that it has examined like transactions of similar organizations and must document any deviations with explanations.

Federal vs. State Laws — Federal law is enacted by Congress in the form of statutes, rules and regulations promulgated by federal departments and agencies, and decisions by federal courts. State laws are the statutes enacted by state legislatures, rules and regulations adopted by state agencies, and decisions by state courts.

Form 990 — See Annual Information Return.

Fundraising regulation — Every charitable organization engaged in fundraising must be familiar with the state's charitable solicitation act. Most states require that the organization and/or professional fundraisers register where they solicit contributions and perhaps grants. This normally means that they file a form and pay a fee. Annual reporting is often required.

Regulated fundraising includes solicitations from individuals; it may apply to seeking grants from foundations and/or other grantors. The IRS is in the process of creating guidelines for online fundraising; until something concrete is available, the Charleston Principles can be helpful for organizations that use their Web site for fundraising.

Intermediate sanctions — Intermediate sanctions provide the IRS with an alternative to revoking tax-exempt status when an organization has engaged in excess benefit transactions. The IRS can impose penalty excise taxes on individuals and organization managers for allowing an excess benefit transaction (as defined above).

Lobbying — Lobbying means to influence legislation. The law defines lobbying either as direct or grassroots lobbying that refers to a specific piece of legislation, expresses a view or an opinion on it, and includes a call for action. Direct lobbying implies that a person or an organization has a direct contact with a legislator. Grassroots lobbying is an effort to reach the public at large and encourage it to contact the legislative body.

Public charities are allowed to engage in a certain amount of lobbying, provided that these activities are not a substantial part of their efforts (or they may lose their tax-exempt status). Because "substantial part" is such a vague term, a public charity may elect a special "safe-harbor" rule. This provides a sliding scale of acceptable amounts that can be spent on lobbying. If the amount exceeds the acceptable limit, the organization will have to pay a penalty tax.

Nonprofit organization — This term, often misunderstood, is useful only in differentiating organizations based on what happens to any profits. In a for-profit entity, the owners or the shareholders are the beneficiaries of any surplus that the company produces. That profit can fill their pockets. In a nonprofit entity, accumulated profit — under most circumstances, also an acceptable and welcome phenomenon — cannot benefit any individual or other person associated with the organization. All surplus must be invested back into the organization, for example, to run programs, buy supplies, pay rent, and appropriately compensate staff. The surplus allows the organization to advance its mission, not make board or staff members wealthier.

Political campaign activities — Tax-exempt charitable organizations are not permitted to participate in or intervene in a political campaign on behalf of or in opposition to a candidate for public office. This is an absolute prohibition. Political education campaigns and get-out-to-vote drives, however, can be acceptable. The boards of organizations that engage in lobbying or political educational activities need to be familiar with the rules regulating such activities.

Private benefit — Private benefit is a broad concept that applies whenever any individual, whether associated with the charitable organization or not, reaps a benefit that is not in keeping with the exempt purpose of the organization. Private benefit does not have to be financial. The IRS does not see private benefit in absolute terms. It is allowable when it is insubstantial or incidental to the main service being provided. It is not acceptable when a service or a financial transaction is purposefully aimed to benefit an individual or a narrowly defined group rather than the public. Private benefit includes excessive compensation of a person who is not an insider and perhaps the provision of a good or service to an individual who is not a member of a charitable class.

Private inurement — Private inurement refers to distribution of profits of an enterprise to the owners. In a nonprofit, private inurement is strictly prohibited. It occurs when an insider — an individual or other person who has significant influence over the organization — enters into an arrangement with the nonprofit and receives benefits greater than she or he provides in return. Insiders — referred to as "disqualified persons" — can be high-level managers, board members, founders, major donors, highest paid employees, family members of the above, and a business where these persons own more than a 35 percent interest. The most common example of private inurement is excessive compensation, which the law also condemns and punishes by means of intermediate sanctions excise taxes.

Quorum — A quorum is usually stated as a percentage or a number of voting members who need to be present to make the meeting legal. To be able to conduct business, a board meeting must meet specific quorum requirements that are normally defined in the bylaws.

Safe Harbor practices — This phrase sometimes refers to what is more technically known as the "rebuttable presumption of reasonableness." This requires a determination of reasonableness by an independent body, reliance on appropriate and comparable data, and adequate documentation of board action (such as in minutes). When the presumption is created, the burden of proof shifts to the IRS to show that the transaction or arrangement is not reasonable. (See also "Intermediate Sanctions" above.)

Sarbanes-Oxley Act — The Sarbanes-Oxley Act affects publicly traded companies and principally regulates the auditors' independence vis-à-vis their clients. It explains the processes for electing competent audit committee members and for ensuring that adequate reporting procedures are in place. In addition, it closes most of the loopholes for all enterprises, for-profit and nonprofit alike, relating to document destruction and protection of whistleblowers.

State corporation laws — Every incorporated nonprofit must follow the state corporation laws. These statutes set the basic guidelines for the board's structure, addressing issues like the minimum number of board members needed, how often the board needs to meet, or which officers are required to serve on the board.

Subsidiaries — A tax-exempt organization may find it appropriate or necessary to form one or more subsidiary (controlled) organizations. This type of entity may be tax exempt or for-profit (and thus a taxable organization). A common tax-exempt subsidiary (termed a "supporting organization") is a separate foundation that carries out most of the fundraising activities for the organization. For-profit subsidiaries can protect a nonprofit organization from liability and/or conduct unrelated business activities that are sufficiently extensive to cause loss of tax-exempt status.

Sunshine laws — Sunshine laws, also called open meeting laws, are state laws that were written to provide transparency and accountability in government. The basic provision of the law requires public institutions to have meetings open to anyone. The laws provide detailed regulations about how meetings should be conducted and provisions for when and how the board can meet alone. While the primary purpose of these acts is to open government to the public, many of the state laws include some types of nonprofits in the provisions. Usually, nonprofits must follow the sunshine laws if they receive state funds, have a government contract, have government officials on the board, or have a board appointed by government officials.

Tax-exempt organization — A tax-exempt organization does not have to pay federal income tax, one of the main attractions of this status. Tax exemption is recognized (not granted) by the IRS. After filing Form 1023 or 1024, the organization receives a determination letter to indicate its tax-exempt status. That is the most important legal document for the organization, and it should be kept in a safe place.

Federal income tax, however, is the only tax that a nonprofit organization can largely forget. It may have to pay certain income or excise taxes on unrelated business income, lobbying and political campaign expenditures, and net investment income.

Virtually all nonprofit organizations are creatures of state law and thus subject to the law of the state in which they are organized and/or operate. By filing appropriate forms, a nonprofit may also become exempt from paying income, sales, use, and personal or real property taxes. For more information, check with the state's department of taxation.

Unrelated business activities — A tax-exempt organization's main purpose is to carry on activities that enable it to fulfill its mission. It is perfectly acceptable to charge fees for services or products. Income tax is not due if these activities are mission related. To enhance its income flow, however, a nonprofit may undertake business activities that are not substantially related to its core purpose as long as it pays unrelated business income tax using IRS Form 990-T.

For an activity to be considered to be producing unrelated business income, it must fill three requirements: It must be regularly carried on, constitute a generally recognized trade or business, and be substantially unrelated to the organization's tax-exempt purpose. If an organization seems to be getting too involved in unrelated business activities, it should consider forming a separate for-profit subsidiary to house the business.

SUGGESTED RESOURCES

Berger, Steven. *Understanding Nonprofit Financial Statements, Third Edition.* Washington, DC: BoardSource, 2008.

This guide will help you quickly understand complicated financial concepts so that you are equipped to perform your legal and fiduciary responsibilities, to set realistic financial goals, and to determine your organization's performance. The third edition of this best-selling title has been thoroughly updated to reflect changes in financial practices and rules. It has been expanded to include practical tips for board members and a comprehensive glossary. It also includes a CD-ROM with a ready-made presentation designed to help your entire board understand and review the organization's finances.

Ingram, Richard T. *Ten Basic Responsibilities of Nonprofit Boards, Second Edition.* Washington, DC: BoardSource, 2008.

More than 175,000 board members have already discovered this #1 BoardSource bestseller. This newly revised edition explores the 10 core areas of board responsibility. Share with board members the basic responsibilities, including determining mission and purpose, ensuring effective planning, and participating in fundraising. You'll find that this is an ideal reference for drafting job descriptions, assessing board performance, and orienting board members on their responsibilities.

Kurtz, Daniel L., and Sarah E. Paul. *Managing Conflicts of Interest: A Primer for Nonprofit Boards, Second Edition.* Washington, DC: BoardSource, 2006.

Help promote a culture of disclosure in your nonprofit by exploring the meaning of conflicts of interest and understanding the legal rules relating to them. *Managing Conflicts of Interest* acknowledges the difficulty in identifying problematic conflicts of interest, and gives recommendations for practice. The key for nonprofit boards is not to try to avoid all possible conflict-of-interest situations, but to identify and follow a process for handling them effectively. How an organization manages conflicts of interest and ensures open and honest deliberation affects all aspects of its operations and is critical to making good decisions, avoiding legal problems and public scandals, and remaining focused on the organization's mission.

Lang, Andrew S. *Financial Responsibilities of Nonprofit Boards, Second Edition.* Washington, DC: BoardSource, 2009.

Provide your board members with an understanding of their financial responsibilities, including an overview of financial oversight and ways to ensure against risk. Written in nontechnical language, this book will help your board understand financial planning, the IRS Form 990, and the audit process. Also included are financial board and staff job descriptions and charts on all the financial documents and reports, including due dates and filing procedures.

Lawrence, Barbara, and Outi Flynn. *The Nonprofit Policy Sampler, Second Edition.* Washington, DC: BoardSource, 2006.

The Nonprofit Policy Sampler is designed to help board and staff leaders advance their organizations, make better collective decisions, and guide individual actions and behaviors. This tool provides key elements and practical tips for 48 topic areas, along with more than 240 sample policies, job descriptions, committee charters, codes of ethics, board member agreements, mission and vision statements, and more. Each topic includes anywhere from two to 10 sample documents so that nonprofit leaders can select an appropriate sample from which to start drafting or revising their own policy. All samples are professionally and legally reviewed. Samples are included on CD-ROM.

Tesdahl, D. Benson. *The Nonprofit Board's Guide to Bylaws: Creating a Framework for Effective Governance.* Washington, DC: BoardSource, 2003.

This booklet includes a checklist of bylaws contents; clarification of the rights and roles of board members, directors, and officers; and a list of additional resources. Sample bylaws provisions and a conflict-of-interest policy are also available on the accompanying CD-ROM.

ABOUT THE AUTHOR

Bruce R. Hopkins specializes in the areas of taxation, corporate, and fundraising law, with his law practice devoted exclusively to serving nonprofit organizations as general or special counsel. He is a senior partner in Polsinelli Shalton Flanigan Suelthaus PC, practicing in the firm's Kansas City, Mo., and Washington, D.C., offices. He has practiced law for 39 years, including 27 years in Washington, D.C.

He taught a course on the law of tax-exempt organizations at The George Washington University National Law Center for 19 years, taught a course on the subject at the University of Missouri-Kansas City School of Law, and currently teaches the course at the University of Kansas School of Law. He teaches seminars on tax-exempt organization law for the Professional Education Systems Institute. He is the founder of the annual conference, Representing & Managing Tax-Exempt Organizations, sponsored by the Georgetown University Law Center.

Hopkins is the author of 18 books currently on the market, is a co-author of six books, and writes a monthly newsletter (as of 2008, in its 25th year) called *Bruce R. Hopkins' Nonprofit Counsel*. Hopkins has been quoted as an expert source for articles in the *New York Times, Wall Street Journal, Washington Post, Boston Globe, Bloomberg News, U.S. News & World Report,* and other newspapers and magazines. He has contributed more than 200 articles to various law and philanthropic publications.

Hopkins received the 2007 Outstanding Nonprofit Lawyer Award (Vanguard Lifetime Achievement Award) from the American Bar Association, Section of Business Law, Committee on Nonprofit Corporations. He is listed in *The Best Lawyers in America, Nonprofit Organizations/Charities Law,* 2007-2008.

Hopkins earned a bachelor of arts degree from the University of Michigan and received his doctor of jurisprudence and master of law in taxation degrees from The George Washington University National Law Center. He is a member of the bars of the District of Columbia and the State of Missouri.